Full Funnel Marketing

Embrace Revenue Responsibility and Increase Marketing's
Influence On Pipeline Growth and Closed Deals

By Matt Heinz and the Heinz Marketing Team

WANT MORE SALES AND MARKETING INSIGHTS?

Check out the Heinz Marketing blog at:

www.heinzmarketing.com/blog

To my amazing family, and our amazing team.

They all leave me speechless...

TABLE OF CONTENTS

STRATEGY

The Difference Between Advertising and Marketing

Advertising is focused on getting you to buy a product or service.

Marketing helps you establish why it's needed.

Advertising tends to be far more transactional. Marketing isn't always so.

Advertising works particularly well in a mature market where need has already been established. Where demand already exists.

Marketing is required to create, sustain or shift that market in your favor.

Marketing can create demand. Advertising can capitalize on it.

Advertising allows you to focus more specifically on prospects deep into the funnel, at the end of the buying process.

But if you're still trying to challenge a prospect or market's status quo, still trying to get them to commit to change or action, that requires a more sophisticated approach to marketing.

The differences between advertising and marketing aren't quite this black and white of course. Just remember that there's a distinct difference between selling what you do vs. what it does. *That* it's available vs. *why* it exists.

There's a difference between not needing it, and not knowing that you need it.

The ABCs of Sales and Marketing Redux

*By **Robert Pease**, Pipeline Performance Practice Lead, Heinz Marketing*

As immortalized by Alec Baldwin's character Blake in Glengarry Glen Ross, ABC meant "Always Be Closing" — Always. Be. Closing.

Wise words indeed and still very applicable to selling. We wanted to expand the ABCs a bit to a few other definitions for sales and marketing professionals.

Always Build Contacts

This means for you as a person and your business.

As a business professional, always work to expand your network by meeting new people, attending events, using things like LinkedIn to make and keep contacts fresh. Keep them genuine and real but make a concerted effort to not only collect business cards, but also have interactions with your network before you need something from someone.

For your business, keep building your list. Your list of contacts, prospects, customers. Use the list size as a metric you measure. Treat it with respect and professionalism, but there is a reason email marketing remains one of the most effective ways to reach people. Just keep the content valuable and the frequency sane. And if you don't send an email campaign to your list at least once per month, you are not doing the minimum required.

Always Build Content

There are so many hungry channels for content sharing and distribution and you have to feed them.

Remember, your goal is to get into the consumption patterns of your target audience and contribute meaningful and relevant content.

This doesn't require huge budgets or massive projects but does require a commitment to building and sharing good content. Think about the issues and challenges important to your customer. There will be plenty of time to tell them about how great your product or service is but master the art and science of speaking to the problem they have and the outcome they are seeking.

Use blogs, contributed articles, tweets and whatever else it takes to reach them but make sure you are doing it. It works and if you are starting from a standstill it will take some time but it will work.

Add these to two? takes on the ABCs of sales and marketing to your approach and remember – keep closing!

You Might as Well Give Up

It's the holidays so nobody is around or answering their phone. Might as well not make prospecting calls until January.

It's January and people are crazy busy starting the new year. Bad time to call prospects or send emails.

It's summer, everybody is on vacation. Can't sell now.

It's Tuesday after a three-day weekend. Everybody is catching up! Can't call prospects today.

It's the week of Dreamforce! Nobody is around, why bother marketing anything to anybody?

It's Monday morning, everyone is slammed. It's Friday afternoon, everyone has already left work. It's.....

Every single day there are excuses. Many are valid, or at least have a kernel of truth behind them.

Of course, if you follow this road, you might as well give up. Give up on your sales goals, your revenue objectives, your marketing plan, your company.

Selling is hard. Earning your prospect's attention is hard. Sustaining that attention is even harder.

But if you want to be around to see the New Year, or summer, or those awesome three-day weekends, you'd better keep moving.

Seven Sales and Marketing Questions Investors Should Ask the Founding Team

Although most of our work is directly with B2B companies and their leaders, more frequently these days we're being engaged by venture capital firms, angel investors and board members of companies who are seeking to increase the efficiency and production of their sales and marketing efforts.

There are clearly countless strategic and tactical questions and directions you can take, and too often a well-meaning but misguided founder will take you down a rabbit hole that doesn't necessarily lead to sales and revenue growth.

I've found that the following seven questions can not only uncover gaps in a founding team's strategy, but also focus and align everyone on what's most likely going to drive repeatable, scalable and predictable sales growth moving forward.

Show me your model

Request to see a copy of the spreadsheet that outlines how exactly the founders expect to drive sales. This should include basic components such as expected sales each month/quarter, how that breaks down by # of deals and average deal size, plus size of pipeline required to hit that number, volume of leads required to develop that qualified pipeline, and expected sales cycle length. You can make the sales model far more complicated than that, of course, but without these basic elements, it's difficult to have confidence that the sales numbers can be achieved.

What problem are you solving and for whom?

This isn't about the product. It's about the outcome. Your founders' articulation of the problem and how its solved is very close to the sales

8

pitch. What are you enabling for your customers? How well can they speak the customer's language in describing the problem? If they can't articulate this without talking about the product directly, they have work to do.

Who is your target customer and why?

Your founders should be able to enumerate their early adopters. What type of companies will buy – size, age, make-up, industry. Who are the specific decision makers internally who need to be engaged? Why do these companies need it now? How does this become a need-to-have vs. a nice-to-have?

What is your sales process, and how does it align with how your buyers buy?

Few companies know the answer to the second part of this question, but it's critical. If you can't align how your customers buy with how you are going to sell, you will be introducing artificial and undue friction into the process. Your founders' sales process should be a manifestation and response to how the buyers buy.

Who is selling for you, and how are you managing/measuring them?

Channel vs. direct, field vs. inside, a combination of these. A specific scorecard to measure what's going on, what the leading indicators of success are in each area, how activities lead to conversations that lead to pipeline and closed deals.

How are you going to generate leads?

Cold calling isn't the best answer, but at least it's an answer. At the top of that model referenced above needs to be an explicit plan for where all of those leads come from. If your founders expect it'll all magically and quickly appear through inbound marketing, you have a problem.

How are you going to decrease acquisition costs over time?

This speaks to making the transition from expensive, short-term pipeline building to long-term relationship management with existing and potential customers and prospects. The better you invest in content and relationships and nurture programs up front, the more cost effective, scalable and cost-effective future sales can become.

This isn't exhaustive, but the crispness of answers you get from these questions (or not) should give you a level of confidence (or not) as to what your founding team might be able to accomplish in the coming months and quarters.

Advice I Would Give Myself at 25

Just a few years out of college, early in your career and life...

If you had just a couple minutes with your 25-year-old self (and assuming he or she would listen), what would you share?

I was asked this specific question as part of a speaker profile and I struggled with the best answer. I'd like to think I've learned plenty in the past 15 years that would benefit that young whipper-snapper. But what advice would be most valuable, most prescient? What would have the biggest impact?

Here are a few I've considered:

Ask questions. Don't be afraid of being wrong, or sounding dumb. The more you ask, the more you will learn, and the better you will be.

Know your priorities, and align how you act with them regularly. Recalibrate as necessary.

Dress better. It matters.

Don't worry so much about your title, position or internal politics. Just keep your head down and work hard. It'll come.

Perception is reality. Optics matter. These can work for you or against you. Know which matter and why.

Stay humble. Pay attention to details. Ask about and remember what matters to other people around you.

Start building and feeding your network now. Just like retirement savings, the compound interest and ROI will more strongly work in your favor over time.

Simplicity is Supremely Undervalued

Complicated isn't better. Complexity doesn't imply greater sophistication, nor does it predict greater success.

In fact, oftentimes, the exact opposite is true.

Is your sales process better because it has six stages instead of three?

Does your landing page generate better leads because it has 10 questions instead of two?

Is your lead scoring more impactful because it takes into account 50 actions instead of 20?

There's a point of diminishing returns in pretty much everything, not to mention the increased margin for error and decreased consistency of execution when you make things more complicated.

Complexity in theory can actually make implementation far more difficult to achieve.

Not to say complex isn't necessary in some cases. Just make sure you're not making success harder instead of easier, more difficult to comprehend vs. easy to understand, translate and convert.

Your Biggest, Most Powerful Competitor is Apathy

Most of your lost deals don't go to a competitor. They go to nothing.

Literally.

Your prospect doesn't choose someone else. They choose to do nothing.

Oftentimes this is for a good reason. Timing isn't right, budget has dried up, other initiatives are a priority. This is going to happen. It's why we call it a sales funnel, not a sales cylinder.

But I guarantee you're also losing deals to nothing because you've failed to communicate the value of translation. The prospect doesn't understand that what you're selling is a need to have vs. a nice to have based on the outcomes you represent.

If you're confusing them with features instead of clearly communicating how you can make them better, they might choose to do nothing.

If you assume that they're translating your story effectively to others who require approval or hold the purse strings, you've lost control of that value translation with the decision makers that matter most.

If you assume prospects got your email, if you assume they're thinking rationally, if you assume they know what you know....you get where this is going.

Unless the cost of change is lower than the cost of staying the same, you will lose. Flip that balance and you'll start closing more deals.

How to Train Your Customers: Six Steps to Better Relationships and Outcomes

I've written a couple times before about how buyers should select and manage their vendors, consultants and agencies. But it goes the other way as well. Consultants, vendors and agencies who don't set clear expectations and "train" their clients and customers up front are more liable to experience friction and frustration down the road.

Whether you're selling professional services, software or anything in between, here are six steps I've found valuable in creating better, more successful relationships.

1. **Ensure a clear understanding of expected outcomes up front**

   Literally define what success will look like. Most often it's a number – but do you agree on what the number should be? Do you agree what you're even measuring? This is a case where lots of people assume – they assume the other side expects the same thing, they assume the client will be reasonable even if results don't come in as high as expected. Better to get those specifics on the table up front.

2. **Ensure a clear understanding of the internal work required to achieve success**

   Too often customers buy something and expect results to magically happen without their input. They expect marketing automation to be…. automatic. They expect agencies to deliver without requiring input, review, or feedback. When these things happen, I blame the seller, not the buyer. It's the seller's responsibility to make clear up front what will be required to exceed objectives – including input, time and resources from the customer. Too often the seller is afraid of losing the deal by exposing how much work will be required internally. But if you win the deal only to ultimately lose an unhappy customer later, was it worth it?

3. **Ensure a clear understanding of the expected and necessary timeline to achieve results**

When you buy something, there's often a level of urgency behind the results you need. Of course you want the results now. Sometimes that's possible, sometimes not. Really important to make sure the customer knows how long it will take to do something successfully. If they're looking for a different answer, it might not be because they have unrealistic expectations – it might simply be because they don't have all the information they need to know what it will actually take. This is your opportunity as a seller to educate, which only serves to make you look smarter and more confident as the right decision for the buyer.

4. **Escalate concerns, frustrations or questions immediately**

I highly recommend that sellers bring this up and reinforce it often at the beginning of a relationship. You may have to force your buyer to voice a negative or constructive opinion early on, but make sure you accept that and make the necessary adjustments to get back on the right track. If frustrations fester, they can create long-term problems and perspections, sometimes without the ability to get back into a productive state.

5. **Ensure a clear understanding of standard boundaries (with exceptions)**

This goes especially for service organizations. You want to please the client, but that doesn't mean five-minute response time for emails on a Saturday night. There will occasionally be emergencies and fire-drill situations, but those should be the exception to the rule. If you start responding over weekends, you'll train your buyer to expect responses on weekends. If you want to preserve your personal time, respond Monday morning and train your buyer to either 1) ask the question on Friday, 2) escalate in the rare condition that it's urgent, or 3) wait. Most things can wait.

6. **Insist on a regular meeting and communication structure**

The cadence and depth will depend on what you're doing, but a regular rhythm of scheduled communication is important. This could include weekly status meetings, Friday afternoon written reports, Trello boards, whatever. Just decide that up front, be explicit about changes made during the engagement, and keep the lines of communication and updates going.

Five Keys to Becoming a Truly Great CMO

*By **Robert Pease**, CMO Practice Lead at Heinz Marketing*

You may have never thought about being great at your job or what it takes to achieve greatness. Greatness is not about power or control but about vision, leadership, responsibility, and accountability. It is most meaningful when used by others to describe you versus applying it to yourself – something that will definitely peg the vanity meter.

Greatness can be defined in many ways...

"To be great is to be misunderstood" – Ralph Waldo Emerson

"The price of greatness is responsibility" – Winston Churchill

Having been a Chief Marketing Officer (CMO) for many years and now actively helping them through consulting work as well as serving as one on a fractional basis as the CMO Practice Lead here at Heinz Marketing, I decided to revisit the topic of what defines a top CMO through the lens of "being great." Venture capitalist and all around great guy Brad Feld served as inspiration for this approach after I read his "Being a Great CEO" post some time ago. So, what does it take to be a truly great CMO?

Be revenue centric as this ultimately measures the value you bring

That this has to be said and repeated frequently is a constant source of frustration for me. If you are working in marketing, map everything you do and every dollar you spend to its revenue impact. Get comfortable with the sales pipeline and what it reveals. Eric Norlin who is both a venture capitalist and producer of innovative conferences Defrag and Glue nailed it by saying marketing is a "...sales person with a budget..."

Constantly try new things through lower cost trial projects

"The only constant is change" is a bit of a cliché but so applicable to marketing today. Not just advances in innovative technology as evidenced through Scott Brinker's (ChiefMartec) awesome Marketing Technology Landscape but massive changes going on in how people find, access, and share information. Real-time availability of information enabled by mobile devices and inter-connected networks makes the art of referrals and brand building a swirl of confusion.

Great CMOs get this and build into their approach a constant test and measure process for new ways to reach customers, build awareness, and drive retention. Do not be dismissive without first trying it.

Replace qualitative with quantitative where possible

Hope is not a strategy and opinions are overrated. Jim Barksdale, the former CEO of Netscape, is often quoted as saying "If we have data, let's look at data. If all we have are opinions, let's go with mine" and emphatically reinforces that data provides clarity where opinions do not. At times, the data can shed light on something uncomfortable or highlight an area in need of improvement. Embrace it. Own it. Now more than ever marketing can be measured in quantitative ways unheard of in the past. Online behaviors, predictive analytics, and a treasure trove of information that constantly flows through the organization about messages, products, and services must be tapped and utilized.

Build the right team mapped to how your customers gather information and make purchase decisions

People make the difference and how you build your team can make or break your time as a CMO. Rather than draw an organizational chart or go with job titles that have been around for ages, look at how your customers consume information and make decisions. Staff to the buyer's journey. If content will drive the sales pipeline, then find good writers that understand the market and build a world-class content marketing

18

organization. If you work in a more traditional industrial market, don't think online marketing including social media are not relevant.

Be transparent with goals, milestones, and progress

The new levels of measurement and visibility made possible by advances in technology and changes in the way your target customers can be reached mean that proactive information sharing is essential. Do not wall off your organization or obfuscate results. If you are trumpeting the success of thousands of leads generated only to have the majority of them fail to lead to sales engagement, then you are doing it wrong. Understand the math that drives your sales funnel including conversion rates between stages, partner with sales on that math and agree upon qualification criteria throughout the sales cycle.

Educate your peers on the executive team, the board of directors, and others in the organization about what marketing does, how you are doing it, and why it is important. As marketers, we often spend all our time messaging outside the organization and neglect internal communications. Each employee at your company now has the ability to have their own voice in the market through Twitter, Facebook, Instagram, Tumblr...the list goes on and on. Arm them with the right information and selectively ask for their help. You'll be surprised at the results.

Use this as a blueprint as you strive for greatness as a CMO and be sure to constantly re-evaluate and challenge yourself. I believe the five items above will survive the test of time and technological innovation but you never know.

What do you think defines greatness? How are you being a great CMO?

Show Me Your Strategic Plan...

I bet you don't have one. Don't worry, I don't have one either.

Ask ten people you respect – people who are hitting their number this year, people who are running sales or marketing organizations and knocking it out of the park – and I bet none of them have a long-term, written strategic plan.

They have objectives. They know where they are going. They have metrics, and focus areas and a disciplined approach to execution, refinement, review, and optimization.

But I bet they haven't written a long-term, strategic plan in a long time.

Gone are the days of multi-year marketing plans. Gone (for the most part) are detailed 12-month plans too (when's the last time you wrote one or actively used one, seriously?).

The world is moving far too fast for those now. Your ability to execute, measure, adjust – all moving so fast now that at best you're creating tactical plans on a quarterly basis. Many marketing organizations I know plan details no further out than a couple months at a time (with long-lead tactics like events being an exception).

Anything more than that, is more than likely going to be a waste of time.

If you plan something for Q1 and it doesn't work, give up on it and move to something else. If you execute and it does work, how much more of it can you do – and how quickly can you do that?

Honestly, how accurately can you really estimate or plan how you will be executing across the board six months from now?

20

Today's most successful marketers work more quickly, more iteratively, with far more frequent reviews and adjustments.

This isn't fly by the seat of your pants. It's still grounded in what's realistic, what's strategic, what's going to drive revenue and sales growth.

Just don't waste your time building a long-term plan that's only going to gather dust in a desk drawer when you could have spent that time making money.

Thought Leadership

Trust = (Relationships + Content) x Reputation

During the Q and A portion of a speaking gig, the question of trust became a recurring theme. How do you earn it, how do you sustain and deepen it, what can companies proactively do to accelerate it, etc..

The more I've thought about this since then, the more I've come to like the formula I jotted down afterward:

Trust = (relationships + content) x reputation

Or in other words, trust is built on a foundation of the relationships you have and the content (in a variety of formats) that you publish and share. The impact of relationships and content is multiplied by your reputation (which itself is often established by earlier instances or leverages of relationships and content).

At the heart of trust is relationships, and personal relationships at that. Those relationships are colored (positively or negatively) based on what you say, what you share, what you do. Your words and actions, your ability to do what you say you will do, your ability to provide value in a variety of contexts – this is all content that impacts your relationships and ultimately your reputation as well.

That reputation then starts to precede you. It represents you when you're not there. You build relationships based on "content" often in a 1:1 context, but that reputation imparts trust on others that may not know you yet.

This isn't a quick process (although it can be reversed quickly via bad decisions).

But I am hard pressed to think of situations where this formula doesn't work.

Two Better Ways to Answer the Question "Who Are You guys?"

When people ask about your company, most of us by default talk about location, size, and make-up. I hear sales reps all the time brag to prospects about their company growth rate, their recent IPO, their recent awards.

Few people outside of your walls care about most of that. And even if they do, it certainly isn't the kind of information that makes them want to learn more, helps them get to know you, or differentiates you in the marketplace.

Instead, I encourage you to answer the "who are you guys" question with one of two angles:

The Founding Story

Is there something unique or special about how the company was founded that blends into your unique selling proposition? Did the founder start the company after failing to find a solution to your prospect's problem herself? Was the company founded on values that align with how you manage the business today, and/or what your clients and prospects prioritize as well? Enumerating a strong founding story can help make your company feel more approachable, and help increase natural resonance with the prospect's worldview.

Your Noble Sales Purpose

Why do you exist (other than to make money)? How are you changing the world? What larger problems are you focused on solving? Explaining to prospects *first* your noble sales purpose is a great way to set a foundation that aligns with both of your needs and desired outcomes. Worth thinking about...

--

When It Comes to Customer Credibility, the Little Things Matter

Let's say you're selling services or products into the residential real estate market. You take the time to understand what brokers and agents need – what they struggle with, how they operate, who the decision-makers are.

You build a messaging framework, a buyer's journey, a sales process. And it still doesn't work the way it should.

A couple small but meaningful things could be derailing you.

Did you know that the term Realtor is trademarked by the National Association of Realtors? That means it's a proper noun, meaning you have to capitalize the R every time.

If your email copy, ad copy, any copy spells it simply as realtor, nobody in the industry will take you seriously.

Similarly, the National Association of Realtors often goes by the abbreviation NAR. But it's not pronounced NAR, in the industry it's pronounced by letter (En, Ay, Are). Get that wrong and you sound like an outsider as well.

The little things matter. Slang, abbreviations, nomenclature. Take the time to learn things like seasonality, industry calendars and highlights, politics. Read the trade press daily. Watch how they talk, how they write, who they listen to.

It may feel foreign, even counter-intuitive at times. But once you look and sound like an insider, your prospect might start taking you seriously.

Character vs. Personality

If you are an introvert, occasionally exhibit introvert tendencies, or know someone in your life who might be an introvert, you should check out the fantastic book *Quiet: The Power of Introverts in a World That Can't Stop Talking*. It will help you be more confident in your introversion, better understand and work with those around you who are introverts, or possibly both.

Early in the book, author Susan Cain talks about the clear shift about 100 years ago from a culture that prioritized character, to a culture that valued personality. It's an interesting comparison and dichotomy.

This isn't to say that character no longer mattered. But with the growth of mass media, those with strong personalities (independent of character) began to gain attention, credibility, and respect.

Character without personality can change the world. Personality without character can win elections and popularity contests, can talk its way into positions of influence, can win headlines and social followers. But personality without character is shallow. It's fleeting. It's actually dangerous.

Those with both character and personality of course can be a force with unbelievable power and potential.

My fear however is that those with high character and potential are repelled by the forces of personality, run the other way when faced with opportunities to engage with superficial personality-driven beings.

Inside your organization, on your team, in your political party, in your family are people who don't prioritize fanfare but who could quietly but powerfully change your world, our world, for the better.

It's hard sometimes to ignore those with personality. it's also hard sometimes to listen hard enough to those with character.

Cost Effective vs. Results Oriented

Sometimes they are the same. More often, they are not.

If you want the best price and the best results, well, who doesn't?

Problem is, you usually get what you pay for.

A lower price up front that fails to deliver its true potential is more costly than most buyers estimate or calculate.

Is it better to get a lower price, or a better result?

Is it better to save a few bucks now, or make a lot more money later?

I get that cash is king. I get that you can often pay less and still get just as much if not more quality.

But too often we prioritize price over value, cost over confidence, bids over the likelihood of success.

It's good to want both. Just know what you're paying for.

Who Gets to Be a Thought Leader?

There seems to be some debate and/or concern lately about who gets to share their ideas. Who should have influence. Who qualifies as a thought leader.

As little as 20 years ago, only a select few people had a voice. It was those with money or access to a finite number of media channels.

Today that's completely different. Anybody with a free WordPress or Twitter or Facebook account can publish, grow an audience, share contrarian views on anything. You can create your own television program via YouTube. Your own radio program via a podcast. Your own newspaper via a blog or newsletter. You can even publish a book without a publisher. We truly live in amazing times.

Of course, this apparently means people who 20 years ago likely wouldn't have earned or afforded a media channel now have one. People you disagree with are far more likely to have access to your customers and prospects and other constituents.

This is exciting and scary.

Plenty of people have access to all of these new tools yet fail to generate an audience. But there are still others who earn that audience to your complete annoyance and consternation.

You think they are full of it. They haven't earned it. They pretend to know something they don't.

There's one way to take away their power and influence – stop listening. But if others are listening, and still more continue listening, that might mean they have something interesting to say. Something that – for some reason – is striking a chord.

I don't get to choose who becomes a thought leader. Neither do you. But together – and with the millions of people in your industry who decide where to focus their increasingly fragmented time – we choose who has influence.

We will never agree that everybody deserves it. But I for one am grateful and appreciative that I get to hear and learn from so many more voices, so many diverse perspectives, to hopefully make my own work (and life) richer and more impactful.

Five Tips to Accelerate Your Target Customer Understanding

Increasing the depth to which you truly understand your customer — what they need, what they're prioritizing and what outcomes they seek — is the key to effective product development, sales and marketing success.

Traditionally, tapping into that insight was time consuming and expensive. It required focus groups, dozens of interviews, and weeks of work to gather a small amount of value.

Today, however, we can accelerate that learning and value with a few smarter strategies and "hacks" with minimal time and effort required. Here are a few that work particularly well for many companies we work with today.

1. Map the buyer's journey

Where did the prospect start before they even thought about solutions? What pain or problems existed first? What observation or experience served to "loosen the status quo" for the prospect to get them thinking that change was better than staying the same?

These and similar questions can help you understand precisely the stages your customers to through before they're ready to buy. And the better you understand these stages, the better you can map your product, your sales and marketing efforts, your content and positioning to walk alongside the customer and help them make positive change.

2. Think well beyond your product or service's sphere of influence

We'd like to think what we offer to our customers is the center of their universe. In reality, most of the time this isn't the case.

What else has their attention? What objectives do they have beyond what you're directly offering? Oftentimes these other priorities have more in common with your sphere of influence than you give credit to on the surface. And regardless of that overlap, the better you can engage customers and prospects on their own ground and their entire ground (not just your sphere) the faster you can develop trust, credibility and preference.

3. Ask "why" at least five times

The questions we ask customers rarely get right to the heart of what they truly care about. The simplest way to drive through to the core need/pain is to ask why. Whatever question you just asked, when the customer gives their answer, ask why. And when they answer that question, ask why again.

This can feel redundant at first, but the extra layers of the onion that get pulled back, and the extra insights into the true motivations of your customers, is almost always worth it.

4. Listen for buying signals on social channels

If you understand the true motivations for your customers – the reason they're seeking change in the first place – you have the ability to filter for signs of these buying signals in a variety of contexts.

You'll often find the first sign of need or status quo change on social channels. Employees complaining about changing circumstances, or the start of persistent problems that will lead to a desire for change.

Use the insights you've gathered in the steps above to start looking for these early buying signals on channels such as social that require little or no cost to access!

5. Talk to your customer-facing employees

Focus groups are great, but the people you can learn from every day are right around you. Your salespeople, customer service reps and others who talk to customers every day can be a great sources of insight.

Remember to follow the "ask why" methodology with them as well to help unlock the true motivations of your customers.

Work the Funnel, but Sell to the Buyer's Journey

It's become trendy in B2B circles to say that the funnel is irrelevant. That it isn't valuable as a tool to track buyer behavior and the sales process.

Poppycock!

The sales funnel hasn't just now become irrelevant. It has always been a poor indicator of how buyer's work. But that's not the point worth considering.

The funnel is still valuable, but primarily as a way of organizing our sales process and helping to direct what we do next, based generally on where the buyer is in their decision-making process.

But it's asking too much of that funnel to hope it reflects both how we sell and how the buyer actually engages and buys.

I'd argue that you need two tools to manage sales.

First, you need a sales funnel that organizes your sales process, broken up into stages, that can help you consistently track progress across the team. This is done based on common definitions, and drives accurate forecasts of future closed business.

Two, you need a deep, consistent understanding of the buyer's journey – how they go through the stages of observing or experiencing pain, clarifying desired outcomes, eventually identifying and engaging with potential solutions, etc.. That journey has general stages, but the specifics are truly unique to each individual buyer.

Let's not pretend that the sales funnel approach means every buyer is engaging in exactly the same way. But if we tried to build a sales process that mirrored each individual buyer's behavior, there's no way we could ever create a consistent, accurate and useful sales strategy.

I believe we need sales funnels as selling tools, but the way we actually sell – the way we engage with, observe and respond to buyer's – is based on an understanding of and adjustment to each individual buyer's journey.

The trick is making those two work together. Your sales process needs to be based on the most common buyer's journey for your target market, but allow for interpretations based on the uniqueness of each buyer's plight.

Work the funnel, but sell to the journey.

What You Do (and Don't) Control

You don't have control of the weather. This might seem obvious, but if your dream client is stuck in a blizzard at the end of the month, they might not be able to sign that contract.

You don't control the quality of your leads – when they're going to buy, when every internal condition will finally be right to close that deal.

You don't control most external factors – market conditions that adversely affect your prospect's confidence and likelihood of relinquishing budget, company re-orgs that put every purchase decision on hold, internal politics that have absolutely nothing to do with you and your deal – but put it on ice anyway.

You don't have control of your boss, your co-workers, your marketing team, the board of directors, your investors.

You don't always have control of your schedule – which meetings you must attend, which trips you must take, which conversations that take longer than they should.

It's easy to focus on what you don't control.

But you do control your time. Your relationships. Your health and energy. Sleep habits.

You control when you get up in the morning. How you take advantage of those early hours. How you set the stage for your day.

You control your to-do list. Today. Tomorrow.

You control what you do next. Right now.

You may not control everything. But you control enough.

Don't let what you cannot control be your crutch. Your excuse. Your reason for failure.

Take what you do control, and make it your competitive advantage. Your secret weapon. Your reason for success.

It's Time to Start Competing Against Your Future Self

What could your competitors be doing a year, two years or five years down the road to demolish your market opportunity? How could they innovate in a way that makes you obsolete, and/or that makes them irresistible?

Thinking about, let alone acting upon, those concepts may seem weird or a waste of time right now. But Netflix started experimenting with streaming video when DVD's by mail was still a healthy business. Kodak, on the other hand, stuck with film until it was too late.

Change is not typically fun or easy. But it's a better alternative to death.

If you don't compete against your future self, someone else will.

Why Your Birthday is the Most Important Networking Day of the Year

You work hard every other day of the year to get people's attention, to initiate conversations, to get someone to follow-up.

Every day that is except for your birthday.

On your birthday, people follow-up with you. It may be to send just a couple congratulatory words, but you have their attention.

I received hundreds of LinkedIn emails, Facebook notes, etc.. I responded to every one of them.

Yes, it took a long time. But among those conversations I was able to get an update from five former clients (complete with a few buying signals), generated three qualified opportunities into our sales pipeline, and started two conversations that may very well become new lead sources for us over the next few months.

It's not about treating that birthday attention as a business opportunity. But I've lost count over the years how often companies and individuals have turned a "happy birthday" (sender and/or recipient) into a revenue-producing event.

Demand Creation and Campaign Management

An Iterative Marketing Campaign Framework

*By **Robert Pease**, Performance Practice Lead at Heinz Marketing*

We often work with companies who are launching new products or exploring new markets and they turn to us to help them accelerate these go-to-market activities. Like with anything new, there is much to learn, many assumptions guiding decisions, and no shortage of changes that will need to be made along the way.

This "test and experiment" mindset is crucial to the DNA of a modern marketer because even with established companies in known markets, the best way to reach prospects changes over time.

I like to use an "iterative marketing campaign framework" to help clients move quickly, learn fast, and improve their go-to-market efforts. "Iterative" because it is a continuous process where each prior campaign informs the next. "Framework" because it lays out a methodology to clarify assumptions, execute activities, and measure results quickly.

Step 1: Identify target opportunities

This includes scanning the market, developing hypotheses related to behaviors and adoption, and focusing on the need and outcome sought by your customers.

Key questions to answer include:

- What problem do we solve?
- Who has the problem?
- Do they spend money on it?
- Do we deliver the desired outcome?

42

Step 2: Create a standard approach

Each campaign needs a value proposition and messaging that resonates with the target audience. You then need to define in what form that message will be delivered (white paper, product trial, webinar, video, blog post, ebook, etc..) and lastly identify the best path to reach that target audience – find out where and how your prospects consume content and put yourself in the middle of it. It could be a sponsorship, email newsletter, or domain specific event but it is out there and there is most likely more than one.

Key activities to complete include:

- Articulate understanding of need

- Structure value proposition

- Create "anchor" content

- Find out where and how the target audience consumes content

Step 3: Execute and Review

Implement your plan and see how it performs. Did you get ignored? Maybe your message was off or too self-centered. Good engagement but no conversions? Check the alignment of your audience, message, and offer. Great conversions but no qualified leads? Right message, wrong audience. They key is to learn these lessons fast and apply them to the next iteration.

Key activities to complete include:

Structure the campaign including budget and program

Compare results to assumptions

If successful – tune the campaign further and repeat

If unsuccessful – move to the next opportunity

The overriding theme with an iterative campaign framework is to have a bias for action and inform the next action with the previous result. Don't spend huge sums of money and invest large amounts of time if you are still learning what works or are operating on assumptions that have not been challenged by direct contact with your target customer.

There are really good parallels to this approach and agile software development. Frequent releases, quick turnaround time, and constant progress vs. large, time intensive "waterfall" releases that happen infrequently and require mammoth effort.

If you have worked in an agile software development company, your marketing team was probably trying to keep up. I know I was in my first one. I learned how to do agile marketing there and am applying those same concepts here regardless of what you sell or how you produce it.

If the Market Isn't Pushing Back, You Might Not Be Pushing Hard Enough

I was called out publicly on LinkedIn for some Twitter behavior I'm not at all proud of. It appears that someone had been followed from our @heinzmarketing account, then unfollowed, then followed again – up to five times.

We use a handful of tools to help us manage Twitter content and followers, as many companies and people do. This includes following people who tweet about sales and marketing topics, but also unfollowing people who go dark on Twitter or who don't reciprocate the follow after a period of time.

That said, the behavior of follow and unfollow cycles wasn't intentional. In fact, we had put in place practices that we believed specifically kept this type of behavior from happening.

It would be easy to blame some of our tools, or our incorrect assumptions around how some of their features worked, or a few other "we didn't know" or "we didn't think through that loophole" reasons.

At the end of the day, if we pissed someone off I take full responsibility for that. Reputations are built in drips and damaged in buckets so this stuff burns me up to no end.

But we (like you) aren't going to please everybody all of the time. Simply because someone complains about your latest email campaign doesn't mean you're going to stop using email as a channel. If someone disagreed with your thought leadership piece, you aren't going to stop writing.

If someone complains about your product or cancels because it didn't provide enough value, you're not going to stop selling it either.

The idea that you can please all of the people all of the time is a fallacy. Even if your intentions are pure, transparent and on (what you believe is) the right side of caution and customer-centricity, I firmly believe that if you are doing things right you are also pushing the envelope, testing new tactics and tools, going beyond what "everyone else" does to create differentiation, growth and results.

In the process you might step on some toes, break some glass. That's OK. You will make mistakes. You will occasionally make wrong decisions. That's OK too.

If your priority is to ensure zero complaints, zero broken glass – you are on a clean and short path to mediocrity.

This is particularly important for a company like ours that is expected to know and deploy cutting-edge B2B sales and marketing best practices for our clients. We regularly describe our own business as a laboratory for what's new, what's working and sometimes what's not.

Great labs do lots of testing, which sometimes requires taking calculated risks. Occasionally those tests make things explode. You either adjust your formulas or abandon that course of action as too dangerous, and/or not worth the effort.

Own and correct your mistakes. Eliminate prospective best practices that turn out to be bad ideas. Define and stick to your values, even and especially when times get tough.

Be bold, even aggressive. But be accountable.

Etiquette vs. Revenue: A Real-time Case Study in "Switcher" Campaign

Stealing your competitor's customers. Not exactly a new strategy, and generally a highly-efficient means of acquiring new customers (since you know they already need the solution and/or outcome).

But how hard do you go after it? How directly or aggressively do you call out how "bad" your competitors are?

If you call them out by name, do you win more customers at the expense of your reputation? Does naming your competitors directly require disparaging remarks? Can you be both aggressive and polite? Where is the *line?*

This debate is happening in real-time, literally right now, in the sales technology market.

Salesloft announced that it was stepping out of the prospect generation space. They chose to instead focus their energy on Cadence, a sales automation tool, vs. splitting attention between Cadence and Prospector, which helps sales professionals generate new leads from LinkedIn.

So basically, Salesloft is getting out of a business that KiteDesk has doubled-down on.

(Full disclosure, Heinz Marketing is a paying customer of both Salesloft and KiteDesk at the time of this writing).

KiteDesk also offers the ability to generate leads from across the social Web, and just introduced several new features that make workflow and integration faster and easier.

So, if you were the CMO at KiteDesk, what would you do?

Does Salesloft have qualified prospects for Prospector that they no longer are pursuing? Are those prospects now actively seeking alternatives?

Do you aggressively go after Salesloft's existing Prospector customers? Salesloft has committed to keeping the service alive for current customers, but that status is by definition now vulnerable.

There are so many ways to approach this. Some passive, some aggressive. Some polite, some scorched-earth.

Every situation is different, of course. But here are some guiding questions I find myself using most often when asked to help clarify or mediate opportunities like this:

Do you want/need the immediate sales bump or do you want to preserve long-term brand reputation? These aren't mutually exclusive, but you may have to sacrifice one or the other. Be intentional about that decision.

Do not act or decide based on emotion. You've trained yourself to hate your competition. But your customers and prospects are typically more rational or indifferent. And they will be confused or annoyed by your emotional response.

Are you willing to burn a bridge with your competition? This is a different question and/or decision than the first two above. You can go after the competition by delighting your prospects, and their customers, in a completely polite way – that still pisses off your competitors. If you sincerely don't care about that, then a whole range of options are open to you.

How widely do you need to share that message? If you're trying to steal your competitor's customers, you really don't need that message to be heard by anybody beyond....those customers. How can you focus and/or limit your message to that audience and mitigate (if not eliminate) its exposure anywhere else?

In this situation specifically, what would you do? Do you take the high road? Do you go for the throat? Is there a middle ground and/or opportunity to do both?

Best Practices for Implementing a Winning Account-Based Marketing Strategy

*By **Maria Geokezas**, Director of Client Services at Heinz Marketing*

As a B2B marketer, if you aren't considering ABM for your business, you probably should be. Account-based marketing, named account strategies, it's basically the same thing. The idea is that you know which companies would be a good fit for your business and your marketing and sales strategies are aligned to laser focus their resources on that particular group of companies.

In the not so distant past, this approach to marketing was not feasible, not cost-effective. There would be no way you could rationalize the spend, not to mention the ROI you'd get from a strategy like this. But now a number of market forces have aligned to make an account-based marketing strategy possible and profitable.

Companies of all sizes make purchase decisions by committee. Sirius Decisions found that over a third of companies purchase by committee, while 53% take a consensus approach. Gone are the days of a single buyer. In smaller companies, the buying committee may be less formal than in large, enterprise organizations. But the types of participants and the need for buy-in are the same regardless of company size. Buying committees are not an enterprise-only phenomenon any more.

It's now common knowledge that buyers conduct most of their research independently, before interacting with a seller. In fact, in a recent study, Forrester Research found that 74% of business buyers conduct more than half of their research online before making an offline purchase. They want to remain anonymous until they've collected enough information they need to feel like they can make an informed decision.

50

Sellers' roles have become more consultative. Information about their products and services are so broadly available that sales people have to be prepared for a more value-driven conversation with these well-informed customers. Sellers have been forced out of their comfort zones of features and functionality conversations and now need to be knowledgeable about broader issues related to the industry, competitive forces and customers' motivations and pain points in order to close the deal.

Technology has made it easier for marketers and sellers to work together to identify buying behaviors and pinpoint potential buyers with very customized and relevant messaging and content. From top-of-the-funnel tools that collect and target the right prospects to bottom-of-the-funnel seller communication platforms, there are a myriad of tools to help companies more cost-effectively deliver their goods and services to market.

None of this matters, however, if you don't have the right strategy in place. And that strategy begins with sales and marketing alignment. Account-based marketing absolutely relies on your sales and marketing departments working together in lock-step. No longer is marketing responsible for the top-of-the-funnel, and sales the bottom. Instead both sides of the organization need to share the buyer's journey starting with a common definition of the target audience.

Both sales and marketing teams need to understand the buyers' motivations and deliver a consistent message. Missteps are amplified in this microcosm, so it's critical that sales and marketing work together.

Get aligned on your target audience

Instead of a geographic market or a demographic/firmographic targeting strategy, you have to treat each company as its own market.

Conduct the research to understand how titles differ between your named accounts. Marketing can conduct the initial research to find the right companies and titles. But then sales will need to validate and add to the research by more specifically mapping the actual buying committee. The sales team can identify the stakeholders involved in the purchase decision, who the influencers are and who has the authority to approve the spend.

Get aligned on your messaging and content

Through the messaging and content that is created by marketing, you need to demonstrate that you understand your prospects' pain points and their industry. Create a library of content that is specific to the target industry. Use white papers and shorter guides to demonstrate expertise. Create email templates that position each content piece for the specific company by using the correct nomenclature and speaking to specific roles.

Get aligned on your delivery

An account-based strategy isn't just an email campaign. Nor is it a prospecting strategy. Instead, it is an integrated approach surrounding your target companies with information that demonstrates your company's expertise, builds trust and opens doors for sales outreach. As marketing delivers the message via targeted web content, email and remarketing campaigns, the sales team conducts their targeted outreach via social channels listening for buying signals, identifying key players and participating in relevant groups.

Finally, as you launch your ABM strategy, it will be important to measure progress both from a quantitative and qualitative perspective. You will want to understand how well you've penetrated each organization by tracking statistics like number of contacts reached and confirmed within each organization.

More importantly, in the beginning you will want to gather input from the sales team regarding the types of conversations they are having with these prospects. What topics are most compelling? How do they talk about their issues? Specifically, what words do they use to describe the projects within their organization? What trends are they paying attention to? This intelligence can then be used to refine the content and messaging for the next wave of outreach.

11 Tweet Chat Best Practices to Increase Engagement, Content and Conversion

To the inexperienced eye, tweet chats can be chaotic and difficult to follow. It's a ton of information flowing seemingly at once, multiple conversations in the same stream. But once you're used to it, I'm now convinced that tweet chats are fantastic tools for both marketers and participants.

If you're not familiar, the basic idea of a "tweet chat" is to claim a hashtag and have a bunch of people talking about a particular topic on Twitter at once. There are several that have been around for years and are highly popular, even in B2B.

I've recently had an opportunity to participate in several, including #socialhangout, #atomicchat and #b2bchat.

Below are several recommended best practices for tweet chat hosts, and a few for participants and guests.

For Hosts

Publicize the featured topic in advance: Even if you're a regular, recurring tweet chat host, let people know what you'll be focused on for each session. Sure, some people may opt out without attending due to a topic they don't particularly care about, but you'll have the opportunity to pull far more people in based on the topic (even if they haven't participated in or have been intimidated by the idea of tweet chats in the past).

Circulate primary questions in advance: Especially if you have a featured guest, give them some questions in advance and encourage them to draft some answers that fit within 125-130 characters. As a participant, it's FAR easier to have these ready to go, to just cut-and-paste vs. try to come up with something on the fly while other tweet chat content is flying fast.

Foster and encourage community leaders and recruiters: You may have initiated a tweet chat for your company, industry or category, but quickly your participants will claim it as their own. And this is a great thing for fostering and growing the community. Identify early those who are naturally leading conversations in your early tweet chats. Give them VIP status, encourage them to continue fostering the community, and arm them with messages and tools to recruit others to you.

Identify and staff multiple roles: Once your tweet chat begins, things can become chaotic. It's important to have a few specific roles enumerated, including the primary chat lead, someone to handle follow-up questions, someone who may specifically answer technical or "help" questions about participation, someone to retweet and favorite participant content, and someone to specifically help amplify good comments through and beyond the tweet chat community.

Use Tweepi to follow participants in real-time: You're far more likely to get the follow-up back if your handle follows someone in the midst of the chat itself. Have someone on your team assigned to this.

Build a Storify post in real-time: Another role on your team can be someone to pull out great quotes from the chat and feature them in a post-chat blog post. Storify makes this really easy, and you can have that post published literally minutes later. Great way to get participants to further amplify the conversation and draw more participants into the next installment.

Capture and repurpose all that great content: As a content marketer, tweet chats might be the most efficient means of collecting a ton of great content in a short amount of time. If you have 2-3 industry thought leaders sharing ideas all at once, you're literally collecting thousands of words of repurposable content in 30-45 minutes. How else can you use this? Blog post, e-book, retweets for days. Get creative.

For Participants

Write out your draft answers in advance: See rationale above.

Turn off other distractions: Tweet chats are busy enough, if you get sucked into email or something else, you're done.

Use HootSuite (or similar) to manage your feeds: I recommend a column specifically for the hashtag feed, a column separating out your own handle mentions, as well as a column dedicated to tweets from the host (so you don't miss new questions or changes in direction of the conversation).

Reply to comments as often as possible: Even if just to acknowledge a point they made, and especially if you are a featured guest.

Use Tweepi afterward to follow everyone who participated: Great way to ensure ongoing connection and conversations after the chat.

Is Your Marketing Penny Wise but Pound Foolish?

Budgets are real, and cash is king. I get it, and as a business owner I live it daily. But sometimes you have to spend money to make money. Sometimes the cost of something is a fraction of the opportunity cost of *not* investing.

Let's say the bank has a sale on dollar bills. For the rest of the day today, you can buy a dollar bill for 90 cents. What's your budget now? Wrong question! If you're fixated on the cost of something, it can cloud your ability to evaluate, calculate and understand the benefit of having it, using it, profiting from it.

That software you're considering isn't just $49/month. It's going to save you three hours a week. What's your time worth? What's the opportunity cost of spending that time on something more important?

Of course you don't need to buy that prospect list. You can have your reps find their own contacts! But how much does that really cost you? Likely far more than the cost of handing them the right list and not only saving them time, but increasing the amount of time they are actively selling for you.

And if you constantly run fire-drill marketing campaigns without investing in long-term market development, content and target market relationship-building, you'll never realize the cost savings, scalability and margin potential of avoiding the premium and "tax" of needing everything right now.

This doesn't make the decision to invest wisely right now any easier. It still costs cash money, and there's an opportunity cost to using that cash too.

But in business as in marketing and life, there typically *is* a tomorrow. Do you want it to be as hard as today?

Check Yourself: 7 Email Testing Tips for a Better User Experience

By **Nicole Williams**, *Marketing Consultant at Heinz Marketing*

Most of us do quick, standard testing on our marketing emails before we send them out. Spell check, layout check, link check. Done. Those are great places to start, but you may be passing up opportunities to deliver a better user experience to your audience. Taking a little bit of extra time to do deeper testing for a few additional areas can influence the way your targets experience your business. The way an email appears when it pops into your lead's inbox can make or break an interaction with your contact, so it's worth it to cover all of your bases before you send that email out into the world.

Here are a few additional things you can add to your pre-flight checklist:

1. **Email Clients** — If you're designing a template (or just a one-off), for the love of all that is marketing, test for a range of email clients. Emails render with great variety (see also: craziness) across different desktop clients—Gmail, Yahoo, Apple Mail, etc.. all have their quirks. But you'd be surprised how many templates get the "OK" before thorough testing, and although they look fine in some email clients, they can really tank in others (I'm looking at you, Outlook). Litmus is a great resource that we use for many of our clients to make sure everything is in its place.

2. **Name tokens**—Make sure your names display correctly, and if you have a default value, double check that it shows up. This goes for values but also for style as well; you won't get the effect you're after if your email starts off with "Hi John,". It's weird when someone says your name really loud when you're introduced. Don't make your email introduction weird.

Note–You'll likely need to live-test this one with a seed-list, as many platforms don't show the tokens (even the default) on a standard sample or test send.

3. **Images** – Do you have alt tags for your images? Not everyone's email client downloads images right away, or at all. Make sure you've got a description of that image that lets the recipient know what your image is for—if your subject line wasn't that engaging, this is your second opportunity to engage.

4. **Fonts** – make sure you're using fonts and fallbacks in your CSS that will display on every client. Some email clients might support more specialized fonts, but not all will. Make sure you've got a commonly used stand-by that will look fine in your emails if your first choice isn't picked up by the email client. Test this functionality thoroughly, too. Nothing worse than seeing your beautiful email show up in an email client marred with Times New Roman. You can use a client testing platform to test this as well.

5. **Spacing** – your spacing will look different depending on what mail client you're using. Some clients have pretty poor support for things like margin and padding, so they might insert extra space, or strip it out (again, Outlook is a troublemaker here). So make sure you're structuring with tables—they're the basic building blocks of HTML for email. You'll save yourself a lot of headache.

6. **Mobile** – This goes back to testing your email on a range of clients. It is no longer enough to check your email's performance on desktops—users are expecting their emails to be optimized for mobile. If they have to zoom in, scroll, or mess with your too-big email on their mobile screen, forget it. In the trash it goes. It is absolutely worth it to spend the extra time (or have a developer help you) to put together a template that's responsive for mobile.

7. **Text version** – As one of your final steps, make sure you've copied your text version from the finalized HTML in whatever way your platform enables it. Preview and clean it up, too. Don't be lazy.

Many of these checks can be done during template construction, which makes it easy and streamlined to deliver a great user experience with subsequent emails that others on your team can build from the template. Add these steps to your test checklist, and you may just find that when your email user experience improves, your engagement rates might as well.

3 Ways to Lose a Lead: Lessons from the #MktgNation Expo Hall

By **Nicole Williams**, *Marketing Consultant at Heinz Marketing.*

Walking the expo hall at a marketer's conference is a fascinating experience—becoming a "lead" rather than a marketer allows me to step back from my own marketing activities and evaluate what I want as a potential customer and what I'm looking for in an interaction. It leads me to ask the question: when it comes to marketing to people who do what we do, do we marketers take our own advice? At the Marketing Nation Summit, it seemed that the answer is: sometimes.

Three behaviors stood out to me that could potentially cost you engagement with your leads, whether you're exhibiting at a conference or planning an email campaign. If you're looking to lose your leads, be sure to do these 3 things:

Don't ask questions

Launch straight into your pitch—that's what they came to your booth for, right? You don't need to know why they're interested in your solution, just make sure they know everything you can tell them about how awesome your product is.

This seems to be a common approach– happened at every booth I visited. After the initial "How are you, have you heard about [insert company here]?" the conversation (if you could call it that) was devoid of question marks. Rather than asking about my needs, problems I was trying to solve, or the biggest hurdles to my success, I was usually treated to short prepared speeches or demos. I left feeling as if they didn't understand my specific business needs and weren't interested in helping me find the best solution.

Takeaway: *Talk about your prospect instead of your product. Find out what keeps them up at night and what about their business is painful. This gives you chance to make a connection, to build trust, and to have a conversation that focuses on enabling them to be successful. You'll build a foundation for a partnership and customer advocacy down the line.*

Talk only about your solution and what it does

You don't need to address the larger questions your prospects are struggling with today–be laser focused on your product. We're only interested in the cool features, anyway.

Everyone who's looking for solutions obviously has broader issues they're trying to address. A list of a product's features doesn't tell me whether this is the right tool for me; successful marketers are using technology to support strategy, not the other way around. So in order to make smart decisions and use the right tools, we need to know what broader questions these tools can answer, what best practices they support, and how it will enable us to make our strategies smarter, more efficient, and more cost effective.

Takeaway: *Give your prospect context on the "why" instead of the "how". Have a conversation about the larger issues your prospect is struggling to address in their space and what challenges the industry is facing. Communicate that you understand their pain and that you have information that is relevant to the hurdles of their work. Make yourself their advocate.*

Treat everyone the same

A badge scan is enough, right? Leads are leads. If someone hands you their card, tell them you're not really the person who deals with accounts, you're just here to tell me about the product.

This did happen to me. I was very interested in how a solution might be adapted for use for our clients, so I offered my business card to continue the dialogue after the event. It was akin to handing a crucifix to a vampire. The rep cringed and reluctantly took it, saying they weren't really the one who deals with follow up, but they'd try to pass it on to someone who does. In addition to making me feel foolish, this interaction told me two things: 1) this company wasn't actually interested in having a real conversation with me about their solution, they were just there for the leads, and 2) lead quality wasn't a priority to their team.

Takeaway: *Not all leads are equal. Prioritize leads based on activity, and pay attention to signals of engagement (like volunteering contact info). You'll be better able to deliver more relevant messages and meet your leads' communication expectations.*

These ideas can just as easily be translated to the way we interact with our leads digitally as well. Using our touches (whether in-person or through email or any other channel) as conversation rather than a pitch can build trust. Listening and responding to what your lead is saying creates a dialogue that will give you the direct path to giving them what they're really looking for and to making them as successful as they can be. And then, when they're ready to put money down on a solution that meets their needs, they'll come to you first.

Inbound-Only Marketing is like Waiting for the Phone to Ring

I've built my business on inbound marketing. It works. But it also has its limits.

By focusing on inbound marketing alone, you have little control over the growth rate and consistency of that growth over time. You have less control over the quality of inbound requests and prospects. The phone will ring often, but you're still basically waiting for it to ring, and hoping there's a good prospect on the other end.

This doesn't mean you can't grow a successful business with inbound marketing alone. You certainly can. But if you want to change the mix of customers you attract, if you want more predictability and accuracy in hitting a particular revenue number, inbound alone likely won't get you there.

I've seen this limit both with clients and with our own business. Thanks to almost 2,000 blog posts and counting on our site, we see significant daily traffic and leads. But if we map those inbound leads against our "target profile" for new customers, the overlap is small.

That organic growth has turned a one-person consultancy into a fast-growing agency, so I have nothing to complain about and am not going to stop focusing on content marketing and inbound. But to consistently hit our revenue targets and particularly focus on the companies we think are the best fits for our services, we're increasingly balancing inbound with strategic outbound marketing and new sales development activities as well.

Of course, if you're doing this right, you're still investing heavily in precise, targeted inbound marketing to mitigate the overall cost of building the pipeline you need. If you're doing it right, outbound is a supplement to that value with far more precision and efficiency.

Finding that balance for your business is a simple math problem. Know the basic mechanics of your pipeline – how many qualified opportunities do you need to get a sale? How many qualified leads do you need to get a short-term opportunity? Then be realistic and precise about how much of that pipeline (quantity and quality) your inbound efforts are currently providing. The rest needs to be filled with outbound.

How to Crash a Conference When You're Not Really There

I missed this year's Content2Conversion Conference. I'm STILL bummed. Great content, great people – my kind of conference. Unfortunately, I caught the flu bug a couple days before, then my wife caught the same. I ended up staying home.

But I was there. In spirit, in content, and in social.

There's nothing that makes up for not being there live, but engaging the crowd, content and potential customers virtually and from a distance was a close second. Whether you have to make a last-minute schedule change, or if you're trying to leverage more events than your budget allows, here's how you do it.

Sign up for conference updates, sponsor events in advance

Sometimes these go primarily to the registration list, but for bigger conferences there are often separate "follower" alerts, newsletters, party invites, etc.. Search for and engage with them in advance to know what's going on (especially so you can follow and engage from afar)

Follow the hashtag

Early and often. This includes posting, retweeting, favoriting, all types of engagement with those who are there.

Respond to attendees, engage and get real-time feedback

Reply to threads, ask questions, get opinions on what content has been good thus far. People love getting responses especially at events where social engagement is heightened.

Follow everyone in the hashtag 2-3 times a day

Use a tool such as Tweepi to "round up" everyone using the conference hashtag and follow them all. Most will follow you back. Do this frequently each day during the conference to provide near-instant gratification for those live-tweeting at the event and looking for who is responding and following back in real-time.

Watch the real-time feeds

This includes the hashtag feed but also any real-time videos posted from sessions. Great way to get access to the content and engage equally in the online discussion.

Watch for sponsor/exhibitor updates

Pay particular attention to those paying to sponsor the event, who likely have their own break-out sessions, parties, etc.. These are often focal points for online discussions and content from the event, plus often more targeted means of engaging with specific content and those following it.

Send LinkedIn invites to speakers, top tweeters and bloggers

Send personalized invites, but be aggressive. Thank them for speaking, for sharing such great content during the event, etc..

Read all of the recap summaries

Many of these will come from exhibitors and sponsors, but they're a great way to get a few days worth of highlights in a few hundred words. Leave comments too, as that's a great way to get your brand exposed to the heightened readers from the conference who are also reading recaps after you.

How to Know if a Metric is Worth Tracking

Can you take action on it?

Can you make a decision based on it?

Can you change something you're doing based on it?

Does it directly lead to your company making money?

If you answered no to one or more of these questions, the mere act of collecting and tracking that data might be a waste of time.

There's nothing wrong with exploring data to find new insights, but too many recurring dashboards and reports included data that never gets discussed or leveraged.

Take that time back. Less reporting, more doing. If the metric isn't leading to an action, it's keeping you from taking action.

99.999% error-free marketing campaigns (here's how)

*By **Brian Hansford**, Director of Client Services at Heinz Marketing*

Every marketing team should target perfect execution of marketing campaigns. Shoot for at least Five-9's of error-free campaigns every year! For the non-IT folks, that's a reference to 99.999% reliability.

Review Procedures

Do you have a quality review and approval process for your marketing campaigns? I have recently witnessed several B2B campaigns that clearly lacked any kind of QA process before going live. Emails with misspelled words, the wrong content served up, inappropriate comments in social media – it's all happened and it's all avoidable. Even the big enterprise organizations are taking short cuts and missing QA review and approval procedures.

New marketing technologies make review processes even more critical simply because of the breadth and depth of consequences from errors. Can you imagine sending an email to your entire global database when it was only intended for a small segment of contacts? What about sending a production email that has "TEST" in the subject line and the field inserts show someone else's name? How about a landing page form that is broken and doesn't allow entries and prevents content delivery? How about a targeted account campaign that features images of one of their competitor's products? Each of these are examples of real world mistakes that could have been prevented with tight QA review procedures.

Here are some ideas to review and test the elements of your marketing campaigns.

Asset Review

Assets include any piece of content, email, landing page that is part of an overall campaign. Here are some suggestions for a review and approval process.

1. Fresh Eyes Review – Do a Copy and editorial review by someone other than author. Includes spell check, grammar.

2. Update Changes – Re-review after changes from first step.

3. Context Review – Ask, "Will the imagery and content resonate with the intended audience, or turn them off?"

4. Legal and Compliance Review and Approval – Do (if required)

5. Final Approval – Get from manager or team manager

Top Tip! *Never ever rely on your own set of eyes to review assets you created! A fresh set of eyes will catch details that authors/creators will likely miss.*

Systems Review

1. Review all of the digital and systems components of a campaign including email, landing pages, forms, segments, integrations and workflow.

2. Segmentation – make sure the correct segment is selected. A large database may take several minutes or hours to build the final segment. Do NOT execute a campaign until the segment build is fully complete.

3. Layout and Rendering Reviews – Use tools like Litmus to test how well emails and landing pages will render across platforms and devices. An HTML email that renders well in your personal email

client may look atrocious on a mobile device. Different versions of MS Outlook are notorious for inconsistent email rendering. TEST!

4. Asset Editorial Review – check all asset builds like email and landing pages to eliminate spelling and grammar errors.

5. Check HTML and Text email versions – Don't count on your email or marketing automation platform to correctly compile a text email from an HTML version.

6. Test all links!

7. Test forms and landing pages – Do they redirect properly and serve the right content?

8. Test programs with a closed seed list to review rendering, readability, and link performance.

9. FRESH EYES Review. Always get a fresh set of eyes to review the program.

These are general ideas to minimize the risk of errors to get toward 99.999% of error-free campaigns.

Content Strategy

Your Content Sucks Because You've Been Neglecting Your Editorial Calendar...

It's been said that the only thing worse than not having a blog, is having a blog you don't consistently post on. For those blogs that struggle with consistency, an editorial calendar is the perfect solution to get back on track. Once the editorial calendar is set up, it's easy to follow, and to maintain. The hardest part is getting through the initial setup and brainstorm.

Getting started

Before you get started on the calendar itself, think about your goals. What are your goals for writing and maintaining a blog? This will play an important part in the development of your blogs' themes, the frequency you post and the mediums or outside sources you rely on. Keep this in mind throughout the development of the editorial calendar. Your goals are a driving force and should be top of mind in this process.

Map your calendar out

According to Hubspot, companies that published 16+ blog posts per month got almost 3.5x more traffic than companies that published between 0-4 monthly posts. That means for maximum visibility and engagement, you should be writing about 4 blogs a week. However, if you're just starting to get into a rhythm on your blog, it might be too ambitious to start that high. Maybe try 2-3 a week until you're comfortable bumping the number up to a higher frequency.

Tip: Some of the details your calendar should include are as follows: monthly content theme, blog topic, blog main points, keywords to include, target audience, due date and goals if you have them.

Brainstorm

The best editorial calendars are mapped to monthly or quarterly themes. If you can organize your blog content around specified themes, the actual posts themselves will come naturally. It also helps to tailor your audience and keep them hooked for a set amount of time; Build your credibility in the industry while making your life a little simpler.

In order to pick the right themes, it's helpful to look into current industry trends or trending topics. Picking a theme that isn't interesting anymore or is a little dated can be tough to write about. Especially, if you aren't already a well-known writer because your perspective on this dated topic will get lost among the crowd.

Plan ahead

When you map your calendar out with themes and topics, plan ahead. Make sure you have 2 months' worth of posts mapped out. After a month passes, update the editorial calendar so you have the following month's posts outlined. It will initially take time each month to brainstorm the following months' posts, but it's worth it in the end because it'll keep your blog posting at a steady pace.

Include all of the details

The most time consuming part of the whole editorial calendar is filling in all of the details. Like mentioned above, including the theme, topic, main points, keywords, etc.. is all very important to a successful editorial calendar. If you include a mini outline of details now, you'll have an easier time drafting the post in the future. Getting a blog title down on paper is great and all, but the meat of the article is the main points. Write the main points first. The title should follow naturally.

Content marketing is dynamic and constantly changing. Last year, podcasts made a comeback and some bloggers even replaced some of their written content with podcasts. It's constantly changing which means your editorial calendar needs to be flexible. It needs to be organized enough that you feel comfortable, but it also needs to be relaxed enough that you can move things around, or add in pieces here or there.

Your readers are ultimately the ones who determine your success. Keep that in mind when you're planning out your content this year.

Circling Percentages with Colors Doesn't Equal an Infographic

It's clear that the past 12 months has seen an increasing diversification of content formats and channels for B2B marketers. Whereas most companies begin with the venerable written blog post, most are diversifying into video, podcasts, Blab events, live chats and more.

Infographics have been around for far longer than when some marketers claimed to have invented them a few years ago. At its purest essence, I think of infographics as leveraging visuals to more effectively and quickly communicate information that is either complex, dense or more difficult and time-consuming to understand in other formats.

Take subway maps, for example. Many subway systems are unbelievably complex. A literal map of their twists and turns and byways would be near impossible to interpret. A written list wouldn't be much better.

So there's been incredible design innovation in subway maps around the world (as well as some absolutely terrible design).

But creating clarity out of chaos is the whole point. Our CMO practice director recently defined a good infographic as simply "information provided in an illustrated manner to facilitate understanding." Taken a level deeper, I take that to mean giving me insights that would take longer and/or far greater brain power to understand without visuals.

We could probably spend a lot of time dissecting those good and bad subway maps to extract a more precise set of best practices for infographic designers. But in the meantime, consider the following questions as guidance:

What is the main takeaway of this information, and how do I reinforce and/or enhance its memorability with design?

How do I use design to heighten understanding of the key points of this information?

What noise can be eliminated to heighten awareness and absorption of the key information?

What takeaway or action do I want the information consumer to have and to take, and how does my design help them get there faster?

Content Marketing Metrics You Should Be Measuring on Your Blog

By **Rebecca Smith**, *Marketing Coordinator at Heinz Marketing*

Maintaining a consistent blog is a vital piece in your content marketing strategy. Content development shouldn't just be saved for informative whitepapers, snazzy infographics or tip-filled e-books. Actually, your blog may or may not be your most important piece if done well. That's why it's so important to continue to track and monitor your efforts throughout its lifetime.

I like to look at blog reporting in three parts: performance, engagement and channel source. I know there are so many other areas that should be measured, but to keep my head on straight, I've narrowed it down to these three. (Content marketers out there— don't kill me for simplifying so much!)

Performance and Retention—is my blog even being read?

Visits: the number of visits to your blog is important to understand who's actually interested in reading your stuff. And, if you can tell where your readers came from, even better. Understanding if they came in via social, organic search, or whatever channel you broadcasted through can tell you a lot about your audience.

Return visits: If your visitors are mostly return visitors, then you're starting to build that base of followers who like your ideas. That's awesome! If they are mostly new visitors, it means you're content promotion is working. Either way, continue to watch this number.

Bounce rate: If the content you're writing resonates with your readers, your bounce rate should be pretty low. If it's high, maybe change up your subject line or make sure your meta-data is on target with the topic of your blog so Google can keep up with your SEO.

Time on blog: If the average time on your blog is low, start picking topics that are trending. The content you're writing about must not be super invigorating for your readers or target audience. So, change it.

Engagement metrics—do readers even like it?

Social shares: If your blog is constantly being shipped off by others on social accounts like Twitter, LinkedIn or Facebook, you're doing something right. Keep it up! Which source is your blog getting picked up on most? It could tell you a little something about your audience...

Conversion: Does your blog sidebar have offers? Are you tracking to see how many people are actually following them through and downloading your other content? One of the reasons for your blog is to build credibility online. Build credibility with your free content and eventually your blog sidebar offers will start to get some attention and capture contact info from your readers.

Source—where are they reading it?

Channel: It really does make a difference if your readers are viewing your content online or on mobile. If it's all online, there's no harm in writing longer articles with meaty substance. However, if it's mobile, most readers will abandon if the scrolling goes on too long. This can help you to determine what type of content should be creating.

According to DemandMetric, content marketing generates approximately three times as many leads as traditional marketing. It also costs about 62% less than traditional marketing... Content marketing is a powerful tool when done correctly. The ROI when it works is priceless. It just takes a little TLC—tender, love and care—and you'll have some content to brag about in no time.

The Suspicion of Value

That's all you really need to get the ball rolling with prospects, isn't it?

They don't need to completely believe you, at least not yet. They don't need to buy into your full story, let alone your product or service.

To get their attention at the top of the buying cycle, they need to believe you might be onto something. That there's a chance, a material chance, you can help them.

Someone described this to me as the "suspicion of value". It's not yet entirely real, it still requires further discovery and vetting, but it immediately rises above other noise as both viable and worth researching further.

At the top of the sales funnel, you just need a chance.

Your Buyers Journey is Too Short

It doesn't end at the sale. Most buyer's journeys I've seen developed recently focus on acquiring the customer, and neglect entirely the process of *keeping* the customer.

What does it take to get to customer loyalty, not just customer acquisition?

How does your acquisition process – across both sales and marketing – set up a long, mutually beneficial relationship?

If you're coordinating the customer-centric story between sales and marketing in the acquisition phase, how are you coordinating that same story consistency with the onboarding, customer service, delivery and product teams?

To start, at minimum, make sure the buyer's journey you're mapping takes into account the path to loyalty, not just purchase.

Buildings Do Not Write Checks

I had the pleasure of speaking on sales technology best practices, trends and predictions at the American Association of Inside Sales Professionals (AA-ISP) Front-Line Conference in San Francisco.

The panel focused on the progression, proliferation and increasingly complex landscape of sales and marketing technology tools, platforms, apps and more. Key on everyone's mind wasn't how many there were, but how we make sense of them.

Which of these tools really help me sell? How can they make me more efficient? How can they do the work for me?

Technology already available today can predict behavior. Automate activity and actions. The machines appear to be taking over.

But on the other side of that argument is that there are real people behind that technology. There are real buyers inside those buildings, behind that predictive algorithm, between the lines of code and cells in your spreadsheet.

Buildings don't write checks. People do. Those people are selfish, irrational, emotional. They don't always act predictably.

Automating more of the sales and marketing process is producing fantastic results for organizations worldwide. Sales professionals can manage bigger pipelines and territories. Marketers can deliver better leads at a lower cost.

But between and behind all of that is, and will always be, your buyers. The story you tell them is, and will always be, central and critical to making all that technology and automation actually *do* something.

Prospects aren't responding to your technology. They're responding to your message. Your story. Scratch that – THEIR story.

It's exciting to know that sales and marketing will always be both art and science. Balancing those, in the face of increasing technology advancements and innovation, will separate the companies that attempt to sell to buildings, and those who succeed at closing business.

Why Your Sales Reps Shouldn't Be Creating Content

It's not that their content wouldn't be valuable. It's just that creating content isn't worth their time. It's just not the best way for them to spend their time to maximize earning potential for themselves, as well as for your organization.

Ask me if sales reps have great ideas for content, and the answer emphatically is yes. Ask me if many sales reps have the ability to create fantastic content, and the answer still is an enthusiastic yes.

But that doesn't mean it's worth their time.

The same goes for social media activity, really. Every solid sales executive I know is telling me they want to see less social and more selling.

But what they really mean is that they want their reps to focus on selling. They want their best, highest-paid people focused on the activities that help them build relationships, rapport and velocity with targeted decision-makers at their best prospective accounts. I don't really care whether you call it selling or sharing or helping or whatever. Your best reps should focus on sales.

There are plenty of social selling strategies that do, in fact, accelerate sales. They can get you new introductions to your dream client, help you get more attention and engagement from early-stage prospects, increase the volume and value of conversations with your best sales reps.

Much of that can be done by curating good content vs. creating it, and you get basically the same external value for your sales reps at a fraction of the time.

Great content drives attention, influence and engagement. It puts your sales reps in a position to win.

Great content is still required, I'd just rather see your best sales reps focus on what they do best – for their benefit and yours.

Six Roles You Need to Succeed with B2B Content Marketing

As the function and importance of content marketing increases for B2B companies, organization of that effort has picked up speed as well. Many companies are developing entire, internal "newsrooms" that effectively mimic the organization, cadence and efficiency of professional journalism environments.

But today's B2B content marketing needs so much more than that. It happens faster, and requires far more work post-publication to maximize impact, conversion and shelf-life.

To be successful in content marketing, you need at minimum six roles. These roles don't need to be owned by six distinct people. In some cases, one person may own multiple roles. In other cases, roles might be managed by multiple people.

But no matter how you organize and execute, make sure these functions are understood and filled.

Voice of the Customer

It's near impossible to create an effective content marketing program without injecting every level of effort with your customer's point of view. This includes up-front input into your editorial calendar, an understanding of what formats and channels your target customers prefer, as well as real-time feedback on published content as well as reactive content production and participation opportunities. This role can be filled by a network of customers directly, by regular input from your customer-facing employees, or by a liaison in marketing (perhaps your product planners, research directors or otherwise) who provides feedback, reaction and input early and often.

Strategist

Someone needs to develop, manage and optimize the content program overall. What are our objectives? How are we measuring immediate results and long-term success? How do our efforts tie into the broader business goals, and how do we integrate our work into that of the rest of marketing, sales, customer service, account management, etc..? This role develops the up-front plan and ensures alignment against goals moving forward.

Managing Editor

This role translates the customer insight and objectives into an editorial calendar that directs premeditated, near-term content development and accounts for immediate, real-time reactive content opportunities. This role manages the overall editorial tone, output and direction of the content. It's a hybrid role really, strategic and tactical but focused on delivering results and output that realize the objectives and vision of the Strategist.

Traffic Coordinator

What's due when? What is the production, review and publication process? What happens when? This is a purely and critically important operational role to ensure everything is done on time, published on time, and executed as efficiently as possible.

Producer(s)

Simply put, this role creates the content. Even with a small content marketing effort, this role is typically played by multiple contributors – writers, videographers, designers, etc..

Amplifier

You know what they say about the tree falling in a forest with nobody around. This role is all about traffic. Eyeballs. Both immediate and ongoing. Too often, companies publish something and drive traffic that day, then move onto the next piece of content without cycling through older but still relevant content on a regular basis. Amplifiers are responsible for increasing the initial "bump" of traffic for new content but continuing to expand the long-term shelf life and impact of the entire library.

The 7th (and Missing) Buying Stage That Can Make or Break Your Content Strategy

You're already familiar with the idea of the buyer's journey, yes? This is separate from your sales process, but should be used as a basis for customizing how you sell to reduce friction and increase alignment with your buyer.

The buyer's journey really *is* your sales process. And it starts without you!

According to SiriusDecisions, the typical buyer's journey is made up of six phases:

- Loosening of the status quo

- Commitment to change

- Review of options

- Commit to a solution

- Justification of the decision

- Make the final decision

Most companies engage and focus on the last four. This is your active sales process.

Ideally, a significant portion of your content strategy is focused on the first two. These have everything to do with the buyer's situation and little to do with what you sell. It's all about identifying and quantifying a problem that needs solving, clarifying an outcome that is desirable but not yet attainable.

Great content strategies combine your understanding of the target buyer, mapped to these buyer journey stages, to put the right content in front of the right prospect at the right time.

But if you follow that too closely, you will miss out on a critical seventh stage – a stage that overlaps the whole journey, and includes opportunity to engage before and after.

That stage is simple: it's all about earning and keeping the prospect's attention. Attention can be earned in a number of ways. Yes, it can be earned precisely by an active buying stage-specific piece of content. But your buyers are more interesting, more diverse, more curious than that.

For example, let's say you're an amazing B2B sales and marketing consulting firm. You're target audience is B2B sales and marketing professionals who need help growing their pipeline.

Your content probably covers – well, elements of the pipeline. It points out gaps in your prospect's current strategy, changes to the market that could require adjustments to how they sell or drive leads, etc.. But if you know the audience well enough, you also know they struggle with productivity. They want to learn from each other. They're curious which technologies are worth checking out.

Some of these and other topics may lightly touch on elements of the formal buyer's journey, but they also work well to earn and keep the prospect's attention.

If everything you share is about work, you will limit the number of times prospects want to hear from you.

Your prospects care about results. But they also occasionally care about nachos.

Blink and You've Lost Them: Why No One is Reading Your Online Content.

*Guest post by **Steve Peck,** Cofounder at Docalytics*

I hate to be the one to break this to you, but the majority of your readers don't find much value in your content. That's not to say you aren't producing quality content. Rather most of your readers don't find an answer to their specific question fast enough, and with all the massive amount of other content out there to explore, they quickly move on and likely never consume another resource of yours again.

This is at least one of the key takeaways from the recent B2B Content Engagement Benchmark Report published by my company Docalytics. Engagement data captured during 180,000 view sessions across 1,700 resources like downloadable eBooks, whitepapers, reports and guides indicated that the average reader spends only **2 minutes and 3 seconds** consuming this type of branded long form content. More telling is that the largest group, accounting for **over 35% of your readers, will spend less than 30 seconds engaging with your long form content**, before they lose interest and stop reading, as illustrated via the graph below:

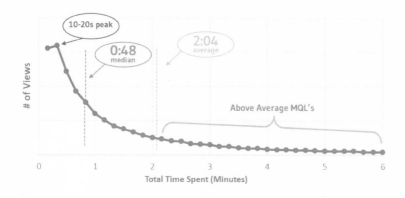

Why you will NOT read much further beyond this line.

At this point we are 174 words into this post, and given the average reading speed for comprehension runs between 200 – 700 WPM or 400 – 700 WPM for skimming *(which let's be honest is exactly what you are doing)*, I have at best another minute and three seconds before I lose your interest forever.

This means it is time in this post to give some practical, tactical advice to not only drive deeper engagement with your content, but more importantly ensure your readers return to consume future pieces of content as well.

Driving Engagement:

When designing content, make sure key stats and takeaways are easily findable. (*Note this sudden change to numbered bullets. Happy coincidence? I think not.*)

Interview experts in your field and include approved snippets of those remarks as credibility callouts throughout your content.

Take the expert advice Neil Patel provided us, which is outlined in the strategically placed expert interview call out box below (see point #2):

How can I design content to maximize engagement? Here's what Neil Patel told us...

Create something that is visual as an image typically causes a higher time on site and engagement. A good example of this is animated infographics... they work extremely well. Sure it takes time to create them, but they are educational and do extremely well from a viral standpoint.

-Neil Patel, Co-founder Crazy Egg, Hello Bar & KISSmetrics

Securing Return Visits:

Build intelligent nurturing campaigns with marketing automation to put relevant secondary content offers front and center in prospects' inboxes.

Say fewer things, but provide ample call-to-action opportunities for those readers who want to dive deeper on the topic or subscribe to receive additional, value added content.

Take the advice Jill Konrath gave us around leveraging your sales team to help distribute your content as part of their value-added follow-up to all marketing qualified leads.

You'll also need to invest in solutions that will help you measure engagement with the different type of content you create. Thankfully there is no shortage of amazing tools to help you measure engagement with your:

Website and Blog Content – While most marketing automation platforms provide surface level metrics around reader views or shares of content, a new breed of Content Marketing Platforms has made massive strides to help you measure effectiveness of your content by reporting more telling metrics such as:

- Attention Time
- Finish rate
- Engagement Rate
- Return Visits

Webinars – The 'pay attention while we talk' nature of most webinar presentations makes it critical that you measure audience engagement. If you manage to get 10,000 people to register for a

94

webinar, and 9,999 of those registrants disengage after the first few minutes, the value of all those new leads will be greatly diminished. Many leading webinar providers now make available metrics that help determine the quality of your content, so make sure you take advantage.

Downloadable Content – PDF eBooks, white papers, guides and other reports have long been a complete black box in terms of understanding reader engagement. More modern marketers now understand the importance of measuring how readers consume these resources, which is outlined in this downloadable content engagement benchmark takeaway published by my company Docalytics.

However you accomplish it, the key is to start capturing metrics around how your target audiences consume your content. This will help you more easily replicate the things that perform well, and eliminate those things that don't. Over time, this will lead to higher quality content that allows you to more quickly build your subscriber base and convert inbound traffic into qualified customers.

Don't be average. Keep Reading.

So we are now 705 words into this article, meaning the majority of your content marketing peers who started this post are already long gone. But not you. You are among the engaged.

So given your interest in the topic, and in alignment with the advice I've given on leaving no dead ends with frequent CTA's, I encourage you to check out our Ultimate Guide to Content Engagement Benchmarks, or if you're tapped out on reading be one of the first to subscribe to the new InsideContent Marketing blog where you'll learn first-hand from some of the biggest blunders in content marketing, as told by the experts who lived through them.

Steve Peck is Cofounder at Docalytics, lead author of the *Ultimate Guide to Content Engagement Benchmarks* and co-creator of the free-to-use PDF Content Tracker. His newest project InsideContent.Marketing features candid stories of success and failure told by experts at the cutting-edge of the content marketing front lines.

Content is King, but Only If the Kingdom is Listening

I wish I could remember who I heard that from. It's way too clever for me to take credit for.

To me, this phrase reminds us of at least a couple things:

Your content can't possibly be relevant unless it's written *for* somebody. Who is your intended audience, why would they care, and what do you want them to take away? What do you want them to do? Don't just write, write with purpose. Write to make a difference. Write to drive action.

Your content won't have an impact unless that audience is paying attention and/or has access to it. What are you doing to earn that attention? Why is your content so good that people are clamoring for it? Who in their existing sphere of influence is going to introduce them to it?

If you don't prioritize creating for and amplifying to your target audience, all that great content planning and execution can't possibly have the revenue acceleration impact you desire.

Social and Influencer Marketing

A Quick Hack to Immediately Increase Your Twitter Mentions

This is fast, incredibly easy, and starts impacting your Twitter mentions (and ultimately your discoverability and follower growth) nearly immediately.

Go to one of your blog posts right now and click the Buffer sharing button or link in your browser.

This will show you what information social sharing tools are pulling from your Web site — which typically includes both the blog post headline as well as other information defaulted in your "SEO Title".

For many sites, what gets pulled looks something like this:

> Ten B2B marketing budget priorities for 2016 — Heinz Marketing http://heinzmkt.in/1MwbAY2

If you're using WordPress, this is likely defined by the settings you have in the Yoast SEO plug-in. You can change what comes after your blog post title to whatever you want, and it will appear automatically anytime someone tries to share your list. I would recommend something like:

> Ten B2B marketing budget priorities for 2016 – @heinzmarketing http://heinzmkt.in/1MwbAY2

This way every time someone Buffers or otherwise shares your content, it includes your Twitter handle — from which they can check out your other content, follow you back, etc..

This should take your Web site administrator 30 seconds or less.

Are You Under the Influence... Influencer Marketing that is!

*By **Rebecca Smith**, Marketing Coordinator at Heinz Marketing*

The best way to get people talking about you is to get with the "in crowd"; someone to vouch for you and give you credibility. B2B businesses are no different. To sit at the right table, it takes dedication, consistency and perseverance.

In the B2B space, decision makers told the International Data Corporation that 95% of trusted peers and colleagues influenced their decisions more than anything. 95% isn't messing around...

To get started with your influencer strategy, you have to find the top dogs in your industry. It can be tricky to evaluate which influencers are the right ones to pay attention to and reach out to. According to a study by Augure, 75% of companies struggle to identify their main influencers. To identify influencers in a certain space, it can be helpful to find people who talk about your industry, look at their social influence, and the cadence of their blog. How many social followers do they have? How active are they on Twitter, Facebook and LinkedIn? Do their followers engage with them? How many times a month are they blogging? If their blog isn't frequent, are they guest posting for other blogs every few days? These metrics will help determine the potential reach your content and leadership could gain by partnering with specific influencers.

There are a few key components of any successful influencer marketing strategy: engagement and awareness, relationship development, and continued nurturing. Think of this like your sales process. Just like you want to develop a symbiotic relationship for your potential customers, you also want to act the same with potential

101

influencer relationships. If you put in the time and effort to prove yourself worthy of your seat at the table, you'll reap the benefits.

Engagement and awareness

Once you know which influencers you want to target, which should roughly be 15-20 people, spend about 30 minutes a day, maybe even less, scanning through their social posts. Either favorite, retweet, like or comment on their social content daily. Repost their blogs through your social channels and give them credit for their work. Make sure you're highlighting where the post is coming from—you don't want to be seen as stealing their content. Plus, you want the influencers to actually see the work you're doing.

Following your influencers' campaigns is a surefire way to get their attention over time. Go organic. Become their biggest fan and you won't go unnoticed for long.

Relationship development

You've been consistently engaging and developing awareness with your influencers for a couple of months now...no joke, a couple of months. This doesn't happen overnight, although I know we all wish it did... As the influencers become more familiar with you and your brand, they may start reaching out to you and throwing you a bone here and there. Take this opportunity to respond more directly. Send a Twitter DM or LinkedIn message, or find their email on their site. Be bold and ask if you can guest post on their blog. Maybe, they'll even want to guest post on your blog or give you an older article to repurpose.

This should take your relationship to the next level. It may even spark a conversation and allow you to share more about your company and the work you do.

Continued nurturing

Just because you're guest posting for your influencers or vice versa doesn't mean you've finished your work. Relationships don't last if you don't continue to put in the effort. Does your new friend have a book coming out, or an event coming up? Help him or her promote the work he or she is so proud of. Continue spotlighting them on social, and continue to share their content. Just like your good friends, you don't use them once and kick them to the curb. This is a mutually beneficial relationship that should be upheld for years to come.

According to the same study by Augure, the most effective content to leverage collaboration with influencers are events (70%). Set up a book launch party to help your influencer spread the word about his or her new content, or organize a happy hour networking event to give her greater visibility. If an event isn't in the cards, try to work on a co-branded piece of content. Any opportunity for your influencer to share his or her opinions and speak on a topic they are passionate about will most likely yield a strong response.

Measuring your influence

Generating awareness, increasing engagement, building relationships and continued nurturing is all well and good, but we're marketers and that means measuring is crucial. If you aren't measuring it, it basically didn't happen. Am I right?

Augure also found that 53% of companies struggle to measure their influencer marketing results. That's a pretty high number. Take a step back and look at the basics you can measure each week:

Number of times you mentioned the influencer

- Number of mentions back from the influencer

- Number of likes/retweets/shares

- New followers since your influencer strategy began

These are good numbers to start with because it'll show your progress. Once you become an influencer marketing pro, you can start incorporating stats including:

- MQLs generated

- Opportunities created from influencer campaign

- Revenue generated from influencer campaign

If you can't measure it, you can't improve it.

Influencer marketing can seem like tedious work when you're first starting out. But, don't be fooled. Over time, it can lead to great connections, referrals, and potentially new business. Don't sweep it under the rug for too much longer, you might miss out on some good opportunities...

The Power of Empathy in B2B Sales and Marketing

Your prospects don't want to hear about you. They want to hear about themselves. We all do.

They don't necessarily need compliments and platitudes. But they do want to know that you understand their issues, their needs, their priorities.

You may or may not have a solution for them, that they need right now. But getting their attention is actually easier than that.

Simply show empathy. Demonstrate not just an understanding but an appreciation for their situation, their challenges, their obstacles to success.

So many ways to do this in a variety of formats and channels.

Filter your communication through an already trusted industry peer who has been there before. Provide a forum or communication channel for peers to share plight and empathy with each other. Learn the language and demonstrate competence not just for your products, but for the prospect's situation. Poke fun at common acronyms, bureaucratic processes and other roadblocks that are hated but tolerated.

Empathy can act as a shortcut to trust if it's done in an authentic manner.

In B2B you're not speaking to a company, a building or a brand. You're always addressing people with heartbeats, emotions, stress and vulnerabilities.

Never exploit that. But embrace it.

How to Become an Industry Expert in an Industry You Know Nothing About

*By **Rebecca Smith**, Marketing Coordinator at Heinz Marketing*

Let's be real. Working for an agency, you come across clients of all different shapes, sizes and industries. You can't be an expert or know all of the tricks of the trade in each industry. That's a lot to expect. But, that doesn't mean you can't learn as you go.

If you know where to look, who to talk to, and what to trust, you'll find it's easier than you thought to become an expert in an industry you know nothing about.

Here are a few ways to become a real authority in any trade:

Read your client's content (then read it again!)

The first place you should look to become an industry expert is at your own client's content. What resources do they already own and what topics do they write about? This should give a good start into what topics are prominent and important in this space. If it's worthy to write an e-book or a whitepaper on, it's probably pretty significant—or at least it was at one point in time!

Collaborate and listen to the client

You've read through their content, so why not ask them specific questions too? They are the ultimate pros and can give you the background you need. They may have hired you to solve one of their problems or enhance their business efforts, but that doesn't mean they don't know what they're talking about when it comes to the industry as a whole. And, if you work together with them, the outcome is generally a lot more rewarding. Ask if you can interview them or send over specific questions you have for them. They'll appreciate the

106

research even if it takes a few extra minutes out of their day to get you up to speed.

Know where to look and what to look for

You could do a quick Google search for certain topics or industry news, but then you don't know which content is reliable and which is lousy. Ask your clients for the sites they use and learn from. What resources do they pull from? Which newsletters do they subscribe to? If they are members of a professional organization in the industry, ask them to share with you their login so you can dig a little deeper into the content they find important. Pull from these resources and you'll get the inside scoop.

Know who to talk to

Real experts love to share knowledge. No joke. They aren't afraid of giving away too many secrets and want people to use their advice to succeed. Who are the influencers or industry pros in this space? Find them and read their blog, follow their social handles, and sign up for their newsletters. They'll have great, first-hand experience that they're just dying to share with the world.

Take advantage of industry blogs

If you aren't taking advantage of blogs, you're kind of dropping the ball. They are the best free learning source out there. You get the info you need, a handful of different opinions, and a bunch of perspectives from a wide variety of experts. Take a look at the different topics or categories each blogger writes about and see which contains the most content. Start by focusing on the most prominent and work from there. You won't become an expert over night, but reading different perspectives and insight can open your eyes to what was going on a few months ago to what's happening in the industry now.

Check and engage in the industry's trending topics

This won't work for every industry, but taking advantage of trending topics via Facebook, Twitter, or any other source you use to stay current, can be a valuable resource. What hashtags are people in this industry using? Which topics are people talking about? These can change daily so checking once a day is a good start to staying in-the-know. It can also lead you to a number of different articles or influencers in the space that will give yet another fresh perspective.

Becoming an expert is no easy feat. It is *earned* over time through hard work, persistence and a go-getter attitude. There are a number of different ways to do the research, and finding the balance between them all will help you become an industry expert your clients will trust with their biggest challenges.

The Difference Between Influence and Expertise (And Why Both Still Matter)

Brian published our list of 2015's most influential marketing technology professionals. It was a popular post based on traffic and social shares, but also apparently a bit controversial.

As with any list, there were those not mentioned who felt slighted. There were also observers who complained about the validity of the Little Bird methodology and the credentials of some on the list.

No list or methodology is perfect. One of the inherent flaws in most of these online lists is that they too heavily weight factors that can be seen online – followers, regular online engagement, etc.. Just because someone is a martech master doesn't mean they spend all day on Twitter!

But this also brings up the difference between influence and expertise. In an ideal world, they would be directly tied together.

But I think we all know people who have massive expertise yet little influence, for a variety of reasons. They may shun the spotlight, fail to leverage amplification channels that could put more focus on their work, etc..

On the other hand, we all know people who have little expertise but massive influence. Those who fully leverage every channel to build their brand but have little below the surface.

In the end, they both matter. And you need them both, but usually for different reasons.

Those with expertise make you smarter. They make your team smarter, your strategies better. They do the learning for you to accelerate your own path to innovation and success. They are educators, accelerators, forward thinkers.

The influencers (independent of expertise) may or may not have the smarts, but they do have a channel that can amplify your own message. Like it or not, if they have influence then by definition they have people listening to them. What are influencers (from a pure marketing perspective) if not channels to reach your target audience?

You can say someone with just a couple years of experience doesn't deserve to be on a "most influential" list. But if they've worked hard to build themselves an audience, why not? If they've earned the attention of your prospective customers, can you afford to ignore them?

Why Are You Following the Leader?

The most common response I've had from people when I tell them I'm not attending Dreamforce is some form of "boy, I wish I could do that too!"

For many, the Dreamforce event will be the most important sales and marketing opportunity of the year. Despite huge crowds, long lines and Uber surge pricing – it's still well worth the hassle and effort.

There are others who simply think they "need to be there." Objections and concerns I hear include:

Will people think our business is in trouble if we don't show up?

If we don't have the same size/presence as last year, people will talk...and that could hurt our brand...

Will I be less relevant to my sales prospects and customers if I'm not there?

What if I miss something?

What if my next big client or dream job is sitting next to me at a break-out session?

All of these are possible. But you can justify away a ton of money and time and effort chasing a bunch of what-ifs.

Sometimes the crowd is right. Sometimes they're just following the rest of the crowd because that's what crowds do.

Your decision to go against the crowd may appear (or at least feel) surprising, unpopular, contrarian. But I bet you'll be surprised how many people feel the same way, and even end up following *your* lead.

By the time the conference kicks off, I'll start to have second thoughts about not attending Dreamforce. I'll see the tweets and summary blog posts, see pictures of friends having a great time at the parties, etc..

But the week after it will all be forgotten. Anybody wondering why I wasn't there will have moved on to the next event, the next conversation, the next opportunity.

As will I. As will you.

Four Lies (And Four Truths) About Social Selling

I was thrilled to join Mike Weinberg and Tibor Shanto for a webinar hosted by Kitedesk, featuring eight specific sales strategies to finish the year strong.

As we prepared our content for this event, the topic of social selling came up again and again, and it was clear that there's quite a bit of misconception and over-hype about what social selling is, and what it really means for sales and marketing in today's environment.

In my opinion, there are four lies about social selling that are causing the most confusion. Here are those lies and what I believe to be the "truths" hidden behind them.

Lie #1: You can use social media as a sales channel

The Truth: There's no such thing as social selling. Rarely if ever can you actually make a sale purely using social as your channel or medium. Social is a marketing tool, not a sales tool. It's fantastic for engaging people, exchanging ideas, nurturing prospects, increasing value-added impressions, etc.. But it won't help you close. It won't help you clarify your value proposition. In short, it won't help you sell. And by sell, I mean close. Most everything else is still marketing.

Lie #2: Social selling is replacing traditional sales

The Truth: Social channels are a tool, not unlike email and the telephone. Social channels are highly efficient means of identifying and exchanging information, but they don't change the way we fundamentally make decisions, how we experience pain and needs, or how we experience the psychology of buying and selling. The nature of the buyer/seller relationship is changing, sure, but that's not because of social media. The tools and process by which buyers buy is changing, but the fundamentals of what works in sales – value, relationships, tenacity, activities – those aren't going anywhere.

Lie #3: Social media leads are warm leads

The Truth: I'm all for building relationships with prospects well before you need them, and well before the prospect is ready to buy. But the implication that social leads are warmer leads, that because prospects are talking to you earlier in the process that they're more interested in moving forward, is fundamentally flawed. Those socially-generated leads aren't much better than your white paper or webinar leads. There's nothing inherent about the channel that makes them any more or less ready to engage.

Lie #4: Prospects are easier to reach on social media

The Truth: In sales as well as marketing, we will always be in search of the white whale. That magic tactic or tool or channel that makes things easier. I'll send a bunch of tweets and LinkedIn requests instead of talking to prospects! It will work better, faster and easier! Not true. Prospects on social are just as hard to reach, just as crazy busy, and just as cold. You will have to work just as hard to earn their attention and respect over time, else they will still ignore you.

Pipeline Management

A 10 Step Pipeline Performance Checklist

*By **Robert Pease**, Pipeline Performance Practice Lead, Heinz Marketing*

We have recently launched a specific practice area here at Heinz Marketing around Pipeline Performance based on what we see as a way to improve operations and increase revenue through an integrated sales and marketing perspective. From our point of view, the pipeline is the ultimate focal point for all sales and marketing activities and accountability.

It tells you where your marketing efforts are being successful...or not.

It tells you where your sales efforts are being successful...or not.

To truly understand performance, you must measure it consistently and over time. But what do you measure? How do you interpret the results and make meaningful changes to improve them? More to come on that but we believe using this 10 point checklist will get you started on the right path and provide some interesting learning along the way.

1. **Understand your target customer**

   Seems like this should go without saying but you'd be surprised. This goes beyond standard demographic data points like role, industry, etc.. and surfaces things like what they read, where do they spend their time, and what are their priorities. Knowing these things makes reaching them with a compelling message that works more efficiently.

2. **Know what a qualified lead looks like**

   A business card is not a lead unless that card was received while actually having a qualifying discussion. Simply having a name,

116

email address, and phone number is not enough. Establish a defined and agreed to set of qualification criteria between marketing and sales and use those to focus lead and demand generation efforts. Don't fall into the trap of creating inflated lead numbers that have to be reconciled with reality as they move through the sales pipeline. Write it down and get agreement between sales and marketing leadership.

3. Emphasize needs and outcomes in messaging

Stop talking about yourself and start talking about your customer's problem and the outcome they are seeking. This should be the rule for everything from top of funnel press activities to bottom of funnel closing efforts. Be an expert on the pain your customer has first and it naturally follows that you know how to address it to get them to where they want to be.

4. Understand your conversion rates

You may have been told there was no math in marketing but we're here to tell you there is and it is the only way to get the best performance from your pipeline. A spreadsheet can be your best friend so get comfortable calculating what percentage of contacts turn into leads and what percentage of leads turn into customers. This helps with planning, budgeting, and reporting. Know the numbers and constantly seek to improve them.

5. Always follow up

Rarely will one email or call do the trick. Actually, I'm going to go out on a limb here and say never will one email or call convert a B2B customer.

Life is about follow up and successful people know this. Lead nurturing and multi-touch sales development processes are, essentially, just being better at follow up and staying in front of a prospect. At a minimum, deliver what you promise when a conversation concludes. Even better? Look at all the meetings on your calendar from Q4 and Q3 of last year, create a list of who you talked to only once, and follow up with them this month.

6. Engage in context

On the heels of number 5 above, do not just send a "checking in" email or apply a "spray and pray" approach to prospecting. Taking the time to consider who you are contacting and what you will say goes a long way. Reference what you talked about last time, how your product or service fits the needs of their business, or something in the news about their company. Take the time to do this. What it costs you in minutes pales in comparison to the quality of interactions it will create. I actually received back-to-back cold calls from the same person reading the same script recently. They had clearly lost their place on their call list and didn't even realize I was the same person on the voice mail they had just called.

7. Understand how your customer buys

It is easy to figure out how you want to sell but have you taken the time to understand how your customer buys? Who can say "yes" but, more importantly, who can say "no?" Be ready for the questions that come up and proactively provide the information that will help move the deal along.

8. Get on the same side of the table

Maybe more figuratively than literally but looking at the situation together and teaming up to solve the problem is a subtle but

118

important way to sell. Sitting across the table and wanting someone to pay you is somewhat confrontational. Sitting on the same side of the table and uniting behind the challenge and desired outcome builds shared expectations and understanding.

9. Get a purchase commitment

This is why we sell and all too often the activities in the pipeline outweigh the outcomes. Understand quickly what it will take to get someone to say "yes," put those front and center in every discussion and methodically work through them so that when you are done there is no other answer than "yes." Don't be afraid to ask for the business.

10. Closed/Won is just the end of the beginning

And hopefully the beginning of a long and mutually beneficial relationship. Keep an eye on what happens after someone buys – are the handoffs to account management or customer care choreographed? You've worked hard to get the customer, so work even harder to keep them. Additional revenue from existing customers should be part of your plan and if you don't formally or informally have a referral program in place with your customers, you are behind.

If You Hate the Funnel, You Probably Don't Have a Quota

Once at an otherwise amazing marketing conference, one of the keynote speakers proudly proclaimed that he hated funnels. He even said he hated people in the audience who liked them.

The idea that the "funnel is dead" or that the "funnel is irrelevant today" has become increasingly popular in marketing circles. It is used to justify a greater focus on buyer sensitivity, buyer control, social selling, inbound-only marketing strategies and more.

None of these are mutually exclusive, of course. And I agree with funnel-haters in that few if any buyers are going to follow a linear process when faced with so many research and decision-making tools on their own.

But I refuse to let go of the idea that I still need to organize and be proactive at engaging with my prospects. The buyer may have more control, but I cannot lose control of my pipeline or my quota by letting buyers simply do what they want, when they want.

It may be popular in keynotes and blog posts to say the funnel is dead, that buyers are in control, that we're not selling but helping now.

But I have yet to hear these words come from someone who actively owns a quota, who is paid on commission, who is responsible for setting and achieving a forecasted level of sales.

Admitting to and managing a funnel can be completely consistent with the idea that buyers are in more control, that the funnel isn't perfect or linear, that prospects can't be pushed into demos and trials and purchase decisions too quickly.

Successful salespeople are doing far more than helping their customers buy. They're finding prospects who have problems they can solve. They're finding buyers whose lives they can change, businesses they can improve.

They aren't waiting for someone to find their blog post or tweet. They're not waiting for the phone to ring. They're being proactive, knowing that there's a consistent set of stages that motivated, qualified buyers will go through to understand, prioritize, evaluate and choose a solution.

That, my friends, is a funnel. It can be completely buyer driven and still managed proactively (even aggressively) by sales.

The traditional funnel may be dead (if it ever truly existed). But long live the funnel!

Beware the Dog and Pony

The traditional agency pitch drives me nuts.

Many of those agencies (across a variety of genres) are actually quite good at what they do. Others, unfortunately, show well but fail to deliver the actual goods when push comes to shove.

There's a huge difference between the pitch and delivery.

Great salespeople can sometimes sell a crappy product, but the company's reputation is going to catch up with them sooner than later.

Bad job candidates can put on a good show as well. They can say all the right things, get your team excited, but if you don't dig deep enough you may find that the facade fades quickly into a bad hire that's more expensive than a couple months of salary.

Agencies that are great at selling themselves *might* be good at selling your product or service too. Or they could just be good at selling themselves.

It's important to root out the difference in each of these cases. I don't want a new employee that's great at interviewing, I want a new employee that's really good at the work. I don't need an agency that's great at the dog and pony show up front, I need an agency that knows how to help me make money.

The dog and pony can be fun, it can make you feel good, it can create a great first impression. Just make sure there's substance to back that up.

And at the same time, make sure you're looking for agencies and candidates and others who might not care as much about the show, but will knock your socks off in substance and results.

How to Convert Business Cards Into an Active Network and Pipeline

Call me old school if you want, but I still love to exchange business cards – especially in an event setting. For me, it's the start of a fast, proven and scalable system that helps me more consistently follow-up, stay in touch and ultimately convert more of those new contacts into partners, referral sources, customers and more.

Of course, feeding your network isn't all about conversion. It starts and ends with adding value, not knowing right away where specific business might come from.

At the SiriusDecisions Summit, business cards will be flying. And without a strategy, those cards might stay wadded up in the bottom of your laptop bag indefinitely. Here's some detail on the process I use to convert those cards into an active network and pipeline.

Ask for a business card from anyone you meet: Let them know you use these as a reminder to follow-up. If they don't have a card, use one of yours to write their contact information down.

Take photos of name badges: Another option if they don't have a card is to take a quick smartphone photo of their name badge. At minimum you can use this to remember and find them on LinkedIn later.

Take notes on biz cards as reminders: What did you talk about? What did you promise to send them or follow-up with? Take notes on cards that can be triaged later.

Collect them in one place: This is important so that no card is left behind. I wear a sport coat or suit jacket every day during events, so there's a specific pocket I use to collect cards (geeky I know but it works). I'd encourage you to do the same – somewhere in your laptop bag, a specific corner of your purse, whatever works.

Process them on the flight home: Working through business cards is a high priority for me on the flight home. I'm typically behind on other work as well, but time is of the essence on those new relationships and follow-ups. The faster I follow-up, the more likely I can continue the momentum of the conversation into something more meaningful sooner than later.

Have a specific "processing" checklist: For me, this includes connecting on LinkedIn with a customized message, adding them to my newsletter list, adding them to CRM, and following up with whatever deliverable I promised (sending a copy of an ebook, making an introduction, whatever). I typically batch these activities, such that I'm doing the LinkedIn and deliverable follow-up first, then the CRM and newsletter integration last.

Set a reminder to review the business cards again in two weeks: This can be done in your office, and is a quick reminder to follow-up on any loose ends from your initial outbound connections on that flight home.

This sequence of course is just the start, but it's the most important part to activate initial conversations and business card exchanges into more meaningful business relationships.

Nine Things to Do Immediately if You're Behind on Your Pipeline Goals

It's almost May. Almost summer. The year is a third of the way over.

You can start the year behind plan. In January. But if it's May and you're still behind plan, the clock is most definitely ticking.

If you're behind on your sales pipeline or demand generation goals, there are few if any silver bullets that will rectify that right away. But here are a few places you should probably look and focus that can often work quickly.

1. Web-to-lead conversion rates

How effectively are you converting current traffic into leads? Are you providing enough off-ramps from your site to learn more, download something valuable, engage with your brand? Nearly every business has low-hanging fruit here.

2. Influencer engagement

The best time to start engaging influencers in our industry was three years ago. The second best time is right now. Treat influencers like a pipeline – you know most won't "convert" right away, but a couple might convert right away (sharing your story and pitch to their already-attentive audience).

3. Trade press focus

Don't worry about the *Wall Street Journal* or *Forbes* or big-name publications. Go straight to the trade press with lower circulation but more targeted audiences. Many will let you write your own column, help promote your gated assets. You'll hear "no" every time you don't ask!

4. Tighten up lead follow-up best practices

Does your sales team call your leads once and give up? Are they optimizing a multi-channel, multi-stage follow-up strategy on those hard-fought leads? Double down on follow-up, connect with more leads at the right time in the right place, more often.

5. Improve your lists

Bad data is the silent killer of great marketing campaigns. It's more than just bounce rates. Soft bounces from people who are no longer the right contact, reaching contacts who have moved on and are no longer relevant, etc.. Improve your lists today, execute the same planned campaign tomorrow and watch your results improve immediately.

6. Empower the sales team to nurture leads, reply to buying signals

Give your sales team better tools that help them increase active selling time. Tools such as KiteDesk, Tellwise, FirstRain and others can make your reps far more productive with a fixed amount of time.

7. Clarify or update your goals

Are you chasing after the wrong numbers? Are your metrics and objectives still relevant? If you're behind plan you need to catch up, but make sure everybody still believes in the same number.

8. Start (or accelerate) driving leads from trigger events

Your best prospects might not bother filling out your forms, but they're still out there exhibiting buying signals and trigger events that are excuses to reach out and engage. Find them, filter them, distribute them to your sales reps.

9. Develop daily and weekly execution disciplines

When you're behind goal, it's easy to start flailing. Doing too much, and not doing any of it well. When you're behind goal, it's more important than ever to focus on disciplined execution. Daily priority lists. Weekly triage and adjustments. Use every minute of every day wisely.

Is Your Sales Process Repelling Qualified Leads? These Do...

*By **Maria Geokezas**, Director of Client Services at Heinz Marketing*

Maybe you've heard about the 3% rule? It states that at any given time 3% of your market is ready to buy (Vorsight).

I'm that 3%. I'm ready to buy. I have a need, and some urgency around it. I did some research to identify the companies that are leaders in the field and then got referrals from existing customers to specific people within each company. I sent each representative an email asking to set up some time for a product tour. This should be easy – right?

Not exactly. On the positive side, it is good to see that these sales organizations are following best practices and have an established sales process to identify, prioritize and qualify leads.

But their sales process is really built for the 40% that are "poised" to buy. This is when a systematic approach is necessary to ensure your sales force is spending their time on the people that are likely to buy.

In the case of the 3%, who are most likely to purchase something, these companies' sales processes actually make it more difficult to buy. Let me provide a couple real-life examples.

EXAMPLE #1

Step 1: Making contact

At one company, it took three days for the rep to respond to my email. It took another two days until we could talk. When we finally were able to meet by phone, the rep didn't want to talk about my immediate need for conference services. Instead, he wanted to talk about a potential partnership.

129

Step 2: Getting a product demo

The sales rep didn't inquire about my timeframe, but I told him I wanted to make a decision in the next two weeks. This timeframe did not create a sense of urgency with the rep. Nor did it help to move things along more quickly. It took another week until we could see the product. I provided my specifications and asked for an estimate. I was asked about a partnership.

Step 3: Securing an estimate

It took another week to put a meeting together with 3 other people to review our specifications. Again I was asked about a partnership. And then it took 2 more days to finally get an estimate. A one-hour long meeting was scheduled to discuss the estimate. We spent 10 minutes reviewing the estimate and then the rep wanted to spend the rest of our time together to discuss a partnership.

Honestly, if I didn't need to present our client with the findings from our research of different conference providers, I would have abandoned this company after the first interaction. They didn't understand or care about my timeframe and they weren't aligned with my objectives to ensure my customer got the best possible solution for their needs.

EXAMPLE #2

Step 1: Making the connection

At another company, I was sent to a BDR or appointment setter even though I had a personal referral into the company. I told the BDR exactly what type of functionality I wanted to see and shared with him our decision-making timeline. The BDR immediately set up a 30-minute meeting with our local sales rep for two days later. I asked if 30 minutes was long enough for a product demo. He said our rep would determine if there was enough time or not. Hmmm… this made me a bit concerned and suspicious.

Step 2: Seeing how the product works

The meeting with our local sales rep did not go as expected. He wasn't prepared to show us the product. He wanted to spend another 30 minutes discussing our goals and objectives and helping to identify our needs. When we said point blank "I'd like to see the product now, I don't want to wait another day to set up another meeting," he reluctantly showed us the product. Only, it wasn't the right product. Apparently, the BDR did not communicate our needs very accurately.

Step 3: Qualifying the seller

Because this company didn't demonstrate that they had the type of conference tools we were seeking, we decided to eliminate them from further evaluation. I sent an email thanking him for his time, but that we were looking for different functionality and would not be giving his company any further consideration. In reply, I received a message that said in fact they do have the functionality we are seeking, they just didn't show it to us.

It's almost like they don't want to sell to me. They are prioritizing their sales process over actually selling something.

Through our research, a couple companies stood out – in a good way. They listened to our needs, responded appropriately and we are moving forward with them. Here's what these companies did right:

At the first company, the CMO contacted me immediately upon receiving the referral from her client. She called to learn about our project, our goals and objectives. During this conversation, she immediately demonstrated her expertise in the area by offering suggestions and best practices. I saw a product demonstration during

131

our first call and received a base estimate the next day along with all sorts of examples and resources.

Another company's sales rep received my introductory email and replied while she was on the beach in Mexico with her family. She understood our sense of urgency and connected us with her boss, who arranged a phone conversation for the next day. The sales manager collected information about our goals and specifications so that when our sales rep returned from vacation, she presented us with a demo that was tailored to our needs. Two days later we had an estimate in hand.

These companies did not let their sales process control their ability to make a sale. Which type of experience can you identify with? Are you a seller who missed the immediate sales opportunity because you are locked into a rigid sales process? Or, does your sales process allow you to flex depending on the needs of your prospects?

Why You Shouldn't Hire a "Head of Marketing"

*By **Robert Pease**, CMO Practice Lead at Heinz Marketing*

People can make or break the success of a company so having the right people in the right roles is a strategic imperative.

Clearly defined roles and responsibilities for any job help align the employee's activities with business objectives and set that person up for success. In situations where there is a new company forming or team being built, ambiguity can rule the day and general areas of responsibility are assigned.

This happens often in startups as the relative strengths and weaknesses of the founding team drive the need for bringing on additional talent. An open position I have seen more than a few times recently is for a "Head of Marketing."

This is not about debating the need for the marketing function in an early stage company. I believe that it is crucial to get the company properly positioned and begin building a sales pipeline to support the business plan.

This is about being explicit for what role you are seeking to fill and what type of person needs to be in it. Having a broad description like "Head of Marketing" signals lack of clarity around what the role needs to do and its place in the business.

If you need a junior level person to own the tactical execution of core activities, then specify that. If you need an experienced, senior level leader to drive market awareness and pipeline performance then specify that.

If you don't know, then take a step back and think about your organization and staffing needs. Casting a wide net with a broad job title to see what kinds of people you can attract and using the interview process to refine the job description is not a good use of time. How can you find what you are looking for if you don't know what it looks like?

Get the most out of your marketing investment by being clear about expectations and responsibilities before you start the hiring process.

Marketing Technology

9 Steps for Building Your B2B Marketing Technology Stack

*By **Brian Hansford**, Marketing Technology Practice Lead at Heinz Marketing*

CMO's and CIO's must work closely to build a marketing technology stack. Scott Brinker's 2015 Marketing Technology Landscape captures over 1,800 vendors in 43 categories. This is exciting and overwhelming! The technologies currently used by your organization and the options to make changes are daunting. With the right approach a CMO can work with their team to focus on the priorities and make sense of the chaos. And the CMO should work with the CIO for stewardship in managing data and supporting the overall stack. Ultimately this focus and partnership will help drive revenue and engage customers.

Marketers have so many choices to do so many things with the plethora of technologies. It's very easy to sign up for services without thinking about data models, integrations, analytics, and the customer experience. There are lots of shiny objects and too often CMO's focus on tactical applications without a vision on the entire stack.

Here are some ideas how to approach building or enhancing a B2B marketing technology stack.

Assess the Current State

Random technology acquisition happens more than we would like to see. CMO's often learn of a new tool or platform that can perform certain tactics or functions. Over time the inventory of platforms grows as well as the complexity of integrations, data management, workflow, and analytics. Tribal knowledge develops on some tools and problems emerge with staff attrition.

136

One of the most common statements I hear from a CIO is that a new base marketing automation platform isn't needed because they have a suite of disparate programs that perform all of the necessary functions. This may be true in theory and on whiteboards. In practice these point solutions may operate in a completely inefficient and ineffective manner due to poor integrations and data flow. What worked five years ago likely isn't right for now.

An inventory of the platforms doesn't go far enough. Assessing the functional performance of technologies is required. Map their usage to the overall business and objectives. An email platform and a disparate landing page program along with a call center program may serve the needs of the business – in theory. But if data doesn't synchronize and flow consistently and customer experiences are terrible, and results are impossible to measure they are not serving the needs of the business. The CMO and CIO must go beyond the whiteboard to truly assess the current state of marketing technology operations.

Map the Gaps and Align with Objectives

A CMO's strategic plan will include business objectives. The assessment will identify what is working and the gaps that require a solution. Be realistic and prioritize where new technologies are needed. It's very important that the CMO and CIO identify the technologies that don't meet the requirements to achieve the business objectives. Again, on paper and the whiteboard a technology may seem OK. In reality it may be time to pull the plug.

The Data Model – Put the Customer at the Center

Brinker's Landscape has 43 categories, which I think can be broken into two camps – strategic and tactical. He states that "categories are a myth" and new categories will emerge or disappear. I agree. And some technologies won't fit cleanly into a category. (For example, Google spans several categories.

CMO's need to develop their requirements for a marketing stack with the customer at the center. This starts with the data model. What are the required data points to capture and analyze? Who are the customers? Where do they come from? Why are they interested in us? How do they engage? What do they buy.

Chances are the company already has some kind of CRM platform in use which captures some of this information. That's a great start and CRM should be the hub for marketing technology. That's because CRM platforms should wrap around the customers.

The Budget

CMO's are increasingly measured on revenue influence. It's wasteful and ineffective to randomly spend on technologies without investing in program design and execution. CMO's that show the impact and influence to revenue will have greater success with their business and careers.

CMO's should focus on planned spending, versus reactive, as much as possible. The CMO should seek the support and counsel of the CFO to work through this process. Opportunities will often arise where an unplanned technology spend is necessary later in the year. A vendor's ROI calculator will prove the value of a tool or platform. But the value won't be realized if the organization doesn't effectively use the technology.

Planning the expenditures at the beginning of the year helps put a percentage focus on the programs needed to drive revenue influence. Allocate and spend wisely, not randomly.

Strategic Marketing Infrastructure and Platform

The marketing stack should support customer data models, the customer experience and measuring results. CMO's shouldn't fall into a short-sighted trap of looking at a marketing automation platform just for email marketing. Marketing automation and CRM form a robust foundation and infrastructure which most of not all other component technologies should integrate.

A marketing stack requires a framework. A framework will help identify the "must have" and "nice to have" technologies. Identify the strategic infrastructure requirements and build the stack from there.

Analytics are a Strategic Priority

The biggest problem with marketing technology is finding efficient and accurate means to measure performance. It's impossible to effectively and accurately measure the metrics that matter when technologies operate in silos and the data model isn't wrapped around the customer.

CMO's should make an analytics engine a top priority when developing the plan for a marketing stack. Many of the core components of marketing automation and CRM have a strong foundation of reporting and analytical capabilities. But, they don't go far enough.

CMO's must develop the data models to capture marketing program performance in order to accurately measure revenue attribution. Marketing automation and CRM platforms offer only limited visibility into meaningful attribution. CMO's need to tell a full story how their effort influences revenue and identifies the right opportunities for the future. Strong analytics and attribution programs provide the prescriptive intelligence needed and they should be a high priority for the marketing stack.

Integration is Strategic (Silos are Deadly)

Many organizations have technology legacies where multiple platforms operate in a standalone silo. This is deadly. Call center platforms and paid search programs that don't capture and measure overall performance will create terrible customer experiences. Silos don't support an efficient customer data model they only provide unreliable data to measure results.

How can a CMO expect to present accurate information on performance, influence and attribution when application silos each capture data in isolation from each other? Data silos were standard in the 1990's but today they are deadly. Platforms must be integrated with the marketing automation and CRM framework. If integration isn't possible, the technology should not be purchased.

Tactical Tools – Distinguish Nice to Have and Must Have

Brinker's Marketing Technology Landscape shows dozens of tactical tools and applications in many categories. Some of these may be nice to have. Others may be a must-have. CMO's shouldn't fall victim to the latest shiny object technology that doesn't serve the business requirements. More technology means more complexity with integrations, data flow, workflow, people skills, and the customer experience. Choose wisely and stay focused on the plan.

Utilization, Management and Administration

Technology enables business processes. But marketing automation doesn't automate marketing. Business processes still need to be designed and implemented. People need the skills to operate and support the platforms. Integrations require vigilance to maintain data flow. There is no such thing as set-and-forget with marketing technologies. A stack requires trained staff and ongoing management and administration. Don't buy what won't be fully utilized.

Move Forward

CMO's will succeed with a marketing technology stacks by following a plan with clearly defined requirements and objectives. Stating "we need a marketing automation platform" or "we need a new email service provider" without a plan will snowball into a hodgepodge of tools and technologies. Look at the big picture when building your B2B marketing technology stack.

Eat Your Vegetables: Five Fundamentals to Kick-Start Your Shiny New Marketing Automation Platform

*By **Nicole Williams**, Marketing Consultant at Heinz Marketing*

Getting started with a new marketing automation platform? Congrats!

So you're all set up and ready to go. You and your team are eager to start building campaigns and sending emails. But before you begin your marketing brilliance, take a moment to set up some organizational processes that will make your life easier from Day 1. Of course there are a lot of great resources that get into the nitty gritty technical details for your marketing automation setup (I strongly recommend digging into these to make sure you're set up right), but I'm talking simple, beginning-stage housekeeping here.

While you're starting your builds within the platform and getting the correct details in place, it's important (and also commonly overlooked) to make sure you're also thinking about the actual structure and organization of your marketing activities – just like you eat vegetables to keep your body healthy, taking steps to organize your platform keeps it healthy, too. Managing your activities when you're just starting out will reduce clutter from the get-go and keep you from wanting to pull your hair out down the road (How did we end up with *two* webinar folders? Why do we have *so many lists*?).

Here are 5 areas for which you'll want to have a plan:

Naming conventions

Deciding on naming conventions will save you hours of headaches for months (or years) to come. Naming conventions make assets, programs, and lists infinitely easier to find, identify, and report on. There's a huge difference between trying to find a webinar campaign that you know for sure starts with "*YYYY MM* Webinar" than wasting time locating a program tucked away in your activities that someone on your team has named "April Sales Acceleration Webinar." There are plenty of great resources out there on how to name items within your marketing automation platform, and each company may have their own formula, but the most important thing is to *do it*, and to be consistent.

At a high level, decide which assets should have leading-date names (think emails, one-time list uploads, etc..), what kind of acronyms you might want use and what they mean, and what order your descriptions will always use. Decide first, document well, and share with your team. Make sure everyone knows how to name campaigns, landing pages, emails, and reports.

A simple structure like *YYYY MM Description Here* works well, but can be adjusted to your specific business needs. If you're looking for more detail, something like "*YYYY MM* EV – Webinar – B2B FastTracks" works well to indicate what channel of program (EV – for event), what specific type (Webinar), and the specific Event (B2B FastTracks).

A note on CRM—it is generally a good idea to keep the names of your CRM campaigns consistent with the program they're associated with in your marketing automation platform. This considerably reduces confusion and creates uniformity across platforms.

Organization

Think about the way you'll want to organize your marketing assets and campaigns—this will need to be a structure that makes the most sense for your individual company. Your business might group assets and programs by region, by product, or by marketing activity—figure out what will work long-term. Like naming conventions, proper organization of your assets and programs makes identification and execution quick and simple. Make sure your marketing assets and activities are grouped together in a way that makes sense, and that

143

similar campaigns or assets are in the same spot. Make it easy for other users to find. If your leads are coming to you from different channels, be sure to organize these programs with special care. Make the distinction between programs that process your online acquisitions, versus nurturing campaigns, versus announcements and newsletters.

This seems like a simple enough concept, but structural chaos often ensues because the initial setup generally only had to make sense to maybe one or two people in the beginning – because they had their hands in it every day. But once you bring in others to help or when you take on a new hire (which will happen), you or someone else on the team could easily break/duplicate/lose something by assuming you'll always just "know where everything is and what it does." So, decide on a clear structure and file tree beforehand.

Sales Alignment

Before sending emails or putting up any forms, make sure you've aligned with Sales on your definitions for what leads are qualified to hand off. Pinpoint activities that make them ready to get a follow-up phone call or email from one of your reps. These definitions may be as simple as clicks on a certain number of emails or as sophisticated as setting up a lead scoring model, but regardless of complexity, make sure you outline objectives for each kind of campaign, where Sales fits in, and how your leads are going to be handed off. Having a documented process for how leads are handled from start to finish makes it much easier for everyone on your team to build comprehensive campaigns that cover every aspect of each lead's journey. This may vary for different types of marketing activities, but the planning process and communication with Sales should look the same.

144

Data

If you have an existing database you'll be importing to your new platform, take this opportunity to clean up your data. Scan your contacts for duplicates, normalize data to eliminate irregularities (like ALL CAPS) and standardize fields like job title and industry. Performing a data health scan up front will help you identify areas where you can append records, where there might be gaps in your data, and give you a fresh start with your new instance.

Maintenance

It's important to identify and de-activate assets or programs you aren't using anymore, elements that should no longer be active (like an event registration page), etc... Even at the start of your marketing activities, make sure you've got a plan in place to perform routine clean-up on your instance and identify areas that need attention down the road. Archiving elements will make recent and relevant marketing activities easier to find and make assessment of running programs that much faster. Depending on the kinds of programs you have running, you may want to monitor and clean up about every 3 – 6 months.

Some of these (or all of these) may seem like no-brainers, but you'd be surprised at how many marketers don't prioritize organization ahead of time and end up with a mess on their hands. The bigger your organization, the more marketing activities you do, and the longer you wait, the bigger the mess. Do your planning and organization up-front. You'll thank yourself later.

Sales Effectiveness and Enablement

The Importance of Practice in Sales

I can't imagine that a professional musician picks up a new piece of music and plays it for the first time in front of a live audience. I wouldn't expect an actor to take a new script and immediately walk on stage.

Professional athletes need the preseason to get back into shape. When new coaching staffs take over and bring with them new playbooks, that means weeks of study, discussion, practice, more practice, etc..

And yet, somehow, we expect our sales reps to take our new messaging, new sales methodology, new product updates – and immediately get back on the phones.

If your sales reps are in essence practicing new ideas or messaging or talk tracks in front of live customers and prospects, you are doing everyone involved a disservice.

If your reps aren't yet comfortable enough with your message, they will stumble...and they know it. This leads to call reluctance at best, terrible and counter-productive prospect calls at worse.

Worse yet, your reps inherently know that taking new ideas straight to prospects on the phone isn't a good idea either. But the vast majority of sales organizations launch new scripts in a quarterly meeting or with a 15-20 minute introduction from a product or sales manager, then shove those reps right back into a live environment to "figure it out."

Sales reps need practice just like everyone else. They need to get familiar, comfortable and confident with the material you've just given them. They need to adjust it in subtle ways to their own style, make it feel natural.

Sales practice should be part of your organizational rhythm. It can be a combination of role-playing, formal practice sessions with managers, or simply recommending and rewarding reps taking time in front of a mirror, or recording their own simulated calls, to get game-ready.

The best athletes, musicians, actors and other professionals worldwide count on consistent practice to deliver consistent performances. Don't your sales professionals deserve the same?

7 Reasons Why Your BDRs Aren't Making Quota

The role of sales development is exploding, as companies exponentially grow the number of sales professionals employed and focused on lead development and appointment-setting capacities.

Simple job right? Find the right audience, identify those with need, and get them interested in learning more.

Of course reality isn't nearly that simple. Yet companies continue to hire aggressively, throw people at a phone and a list, and wonder why they aren't hitting their number.

If you're managing a sales development or business development representative (BDR) team, make sure the following seven symptoms aren't dragging down your results.

They lack discipline

Sales development is a difficult job. It requires a high volume of activity that can typically only be consistently achieved by staying focused on execution for stretches of time. This takes discipline and a set or productivity and efficiency skills that most BDRs aren't naturally equipped with. This training alone – helping your reps hone the ability to focus and execute – can alone significantly increase their capacity and results.

They don't understand your customers or their industry

Sales training too often focuses on product knowledge at the expense of customer and industry knowledge. Do your reps know who they're speaking to? Do they know their language, their slang, their acronyms? Do they understand the calendar cycles of their industry such that they can speak credibly, build rapport, and continue the conversation?

Their lists suck

Lists always suck. There is no perfect list. But too often BDRs are given lists that marketing says are fine, but in reality cause a dramatic drop in their productivity. Those lists may "appear" fine when used to send email, because the resulting response metrics look fine. But if you require an individual rep to call each and every prospect, they'll end up wasting time with a high volume of prospects that don't exist, are the wrong buyer, or take five times too long to reach simply because the data hasn't been updated in forever.

Their pitch sucks

Left to their own devices (and far too many BDRs are), and in a vacuum of customer/industry understanding, your reps will create a pitch that is product-centric. It will confuse your prospects, delivered out of context and in the midst of a crazy-busy day that allows for zero wiggle room to interpret something new that isn't easy to understand. Great pitches aren't about product, they're about people and products.

They lack motivation

Motivation can be simple. It can be $20 bucks in beer money on a Friday afternoon. It can be recognition in front of their peers. It can be the little things that help jump-start behavior and create habits. If you think motivation is "well, they have a job and our comp plan is solid", you're missing an opportunity to not just drive greater productivity but retention and loyalty as well.

They're pushing prospects too far, too fast

"Thanks for downloading our white paper, would you like to see a demo?" Uh, no thanks. You can't ask prospects to sleep with you on the first date. If your primary metric across the sales development team is demo appointments, you might be moving too fast for your prospects. Appointments are fine, but up front they should be positioned based on the prospect's needs, not your product pitch.

They lack empathy and customer understanding

This is a culmination of training and practice. Of listening to those who came before you, and to the shifting needs of the prospects you're speaking with every day. The BDRs that care more about their prospects than they do their products consistently perform better. Even over the phone, your prospects will hear this and respond positively to it.

Why Your Best Sales Operations Candidates Are Former Sales Reps

Some of the best demand generation marketers I've worked with have actually come from the sales side. They spent the early part of their career carrying a bag, owning a quota.

They know that effective B2B marketing isn't about pretty pictures and cold lists and flashy trade show booths. They know that everything boils down to pipeline growth and revenue responsibility.

Former sales pros understand intimately what their former direct peers are going through. They're far more likely to understand and successfully execute on the sales enablement side of modern marketing's role.

A similar rationale could put some of your sales reps successfully into an operations role. If you hire administrative professionals into sales operations, they tend to be too reactive. Too focused on tactics and not results. They don't inherently understand the sales role and how to support it.

That's absolutely not to imply that successful sales operations is a subservient position. Quite the contrary, well-executed sales operations is quite possibly the most important role on the entire sales floor.

A well-run, focused and nimble sales operations group can make every single sales professional more efficient, more effective and more successful. They can single-handedly improve productivity, sales pipeline growth and conversion rates.

In that light, I could argue that putting one of your best reps in a sales operations management role might not only help you retain them but also significantly increase their value to the organization.

- - -

Nine Mobile Productivity Tips for Sales Pros On the Go

These tips apply to anyone who travels frequently for work – and especially for those who find themselves going from meeting to meeting away from their desk. These can be significant time savers!

Carry paper: Seriously, as awesome as note-capturing apps can be, sometimes what you really need is to write something down! Depending on the circumstance, writing a note on pen and paper is better etiquette than pulling out your smartphone or tablet.

Make your CRM available online: Contacts, accounts, notes. The more of this is available anywhere, the more likely you have whatever data you need at your fingertips.

Use voice controls: Control CRM by voice? It's possible. Check out Nuiku.

Organize your apps better: Which do you use most often? Which do you use in succession? Sort them more effectively on your phone and/or tablet so you spend less time fumbling and more time doing.

Use Dial2Do: For $2.49/month, leave yourselves a voicemail and it'll translate that message into text and email it to you. Huge time saver not to mention master capturer of far more ideas, tasks, etc..

Prepare in advance for your day: The night before, make your to-do list. Keep it handy so you can quickly switch to priority tasks when you have time between meetings. Do research on your next day's meetings via LinkedIn, Charlie and others. Do the math on where you need to be first, when, how long it'll take you to get there, when you need to leave your hotel or office or home. Life savers.

154

Avoid distractions as best as possible: Your email will be there for you when you get back to the office. Voicemails too. You're on the road for a reason, focus there and get the job done.

Capture and triage to-do's before day's end: Don't stop working until you've captured your next steps somewhere in a trusted system. Pull them out of your notes and brain before they get lost.

Set up Evercontact back at the office: It'll capture updated contact information from emails in your inbox automatically, keeping your contact list up to date. That way when you need that updated phone number on the road, it's right there for you.

A Quick (and Free) Hack for Measuring Active Selling Time Across Your Sales Organization

I'm thrilled to see the increased focus on measuring and managing active selling time from sales organizations nationwide – both those with dedicated inside sales teams as well as those with hybrid inside + field sales teams.

According to multiple research reports I've seen this year, the average B2B sales professional spends just 33 percent of their time actively selling. The rest of that time is spent preparing, researching, updating CRM, in meetings or training, etc..

Some of that "downtime" of course isn't going away. But even if you can move that 33 percent to 40 percent by eliminating wasteful activity, redundant behavior, unnecessary slack time, etc.. – across the entire salesforce that's a massive increase in productivity and potential new business with minimal cost and zero additional labor.

There are many expensive options to measure a baseline for active selling time across your team. Or you could have everybody install RescueTime.

Yes, there are team versions of RescueTime that will give you visibility into who's doing what.

But start cheaper (read: free).

Designate different applications as active vs. inactive. For example, time in CRM is inactive. Time in email is active (again, generalities). There's an advanced version of RescueTime that can manage offline activities such as phone time and meeting time too.

Using Rescue Time, get a baseline for how much of your team's time is on active vs. inactive selling activities. Then identify the primary culprits of inefficiency and get to work. Worth a shot...

Productive but Not Effective (is a Complete Waste of Time)

If you make 100 phone calls to prospects today but have no idea what to say to them, you've wasted your time.

If you make 100 phone calls but don't leave voicemails, it's as if you never called.

If you take 30 minutes to research your new prospect only to leave a 30 second voicemail, was that 30 minutes worthwhile?

Knowing what to do is important. Being efficient at execution is important.

But there's a huge difference between efficient and effective. You need both.

Do Sales Prospects Buy Based on Emotion or Logic?

It was a fair question, albeit asked inappropriately, during a sales best practices panel I moderated as part of Seattle Startup Week.

We had an all-female panel talking about everything from gender bias in sales to general best practices, how to learn and adjust in different sales environments, etc..

During the Q & A, one attendee asked how women in sales can "adjust" their approach when working in B2B. His premise, which raised plenty of eyebrows, was that consumers buy on emotion and B2B buyers select based on logic. He further opined that men are more logical and women more emotional, and wondered what was the secret to women being successful in B2B sales.

I share this story for a couple reasons.

One, he actually made it out of the room alive. For a minute there, I wasn't so sure.

Second, the first answer from one of our panelists was I believe the right one, and it's a point worth noting in any selling situation.

Rather than addressing the sexist bias inherent in the question, our panelist explained that all decisions in sales are a mix of logic and emotion.

If every decision was made on logic alone, it would be a lot easier to sell! Fortunately, or unfortunately (depending on the selling environment or circumstance), emotion plays a large role as well. Smart salespeople can accurately ascertain the situation, understand the buyer's motivations, and leverage a combination of logic and emotion to make a connection and sale. It's never cleanly one or the other.

There is No Sale Without Marketing, and No Marketing Without Sales

It may be true that up to two-thirds of the buying process is completed before sales gets actively involved (based on research from Forrester and others), but it's important to keep in mind that this statistic is an average. It's reflective of what everyone is doing melded together, on the buyer and seller side, vs. what the best companies are executing on to exceed quota again and again.

New research published last week from SiriusDecisions seems to reflect a more realistic and optimistic scenario, demonstrating that sales professionals are providing value at every stage of the buying process. And, in fact, buyers still request and appreciate a value-added sales professional to help facilitate the right decision.

Yes, buyers are more educated. Yes, they're self-navigating more of the early stages of the buyer's journey on their own. Yes, this means that marketing's role in the buyer's journey and, hence, the sales process is far more important than ever before.

Lost in this entire discussion and debate, however, is the fact that successful, scalable growth organizations cannot and will not exist entirely with sales or entirely with marketing. The best organizations blend those roles together into a single buying experience, a central and powerful buying story.

There was additional, compelling evidence at the SiriusDecisions Summit that sales-driven demand is four times more likely to close than marketing-driven demand. This is often more true, and more material, for larger-sized deals than SMB sales opportunities.

But that statistic only tells part of the story. Although sales-driven demand might be more efficient on a conversion basis, those deals

159

(according to SiriusDecisions research) can cost up to five times more to acquire when marketing isn't involved.

Great marketing makes the sales job more efficient, more predictable. Great sales programs capitalize and convert on great marketing.

I don't see a scenario anytime soon when seven-figure enterprise purchases will happen as a direct result of a white paper download. I also don't see a scenario where serious companies focused on growth will stop investing in marketing to make their pipelines more efficient, today and into the future.

To say that sales and marketing are in this together is an understatement. One or the other isn't at all sufficient. Coordinating efforts is a great start.

But the market-leading companies today and into the near future will continue to treat sales and marketing as a unified, coordinated, tightly-blended effort.

It's not about holding off sales until the end of the buying process. It's not about placing blame, or even about precisely identifying attribution.

Market leaders deploy every resource across the sales and marketing organizations to deliver and reinforce the right message, the right value, at the right time to prospective, current and future customers. Period.

Why Your Sales Reps Need Improv Training

Chad Burmeister from Connect and Sell did a brave thing. At the AA-ISP Front Lines event in Denver, he played recordings of some of his own sales reps' phone calls with prospects and asked a panel on stage to critique the calls.

Cringes and nervous laughter abounded. Trish Bertuzzi from The Bridge Group (one of the panelists) reminded the audience that all of our sales teams make the same mistakes (reinforcing why constant training and coaching is so important).

But what struck me in the audience was just how important improvisational techniques are to a successful sales rep.

There's no such thing as a script for a live sales call. You need to have a plan, have a solid sense for where you want the call to go. You need to know your messaging, and know generally the issues your customer is likely facing.

But coming up with the perfect words in real-time is extremely hard.

Few other people in your business have to act on their feet in this way. Your CEO might have to do it on an analyst call or in a press interview. But most everybody else (including marketing) can prepare their words in advance.

So should we be hiring comedy improv instructors to teach our sales and customer service teams to work on their feet? How do we help reps become more comfortable having semi-unpredictable, real-time conversations but stick to the principles of your messaging and sales strategy?

Worth thinking about...

Three Statistics that Make the Case for Sales and Marketing Alignment

*By **Alexis Getscher** | Content Marketing – Bizible*

Bizible published our first annual State of Pipeline Marketing Report after surveying over 350 B2B marketers on various topics like how they measure success, which metrics have the greatest impact on revenue, and marketing priorities.

In this post, I'd like to break down the results surrounding sales and marketing alignment. Apparently, it's not as cut and dry as I would have expected: Of all marketers surveyed, 68.4 percent said they were "tightly aligned" or "generally aligned" with sales, leaving 31.6 percent as "somewhat aligned," "rarely aligned," or "misaligned." (I've combined the latter three answers into "Seldomly Aligned" within the charts below).

Sales and Marketing Alignment vs. Job Level

In the chart below, we compare marketer's job level to their degree of sales and marketing alignment. Notably, 72.6 percent of those who answered within the category seldomly aligned with sales fell into the job levels of middle management and under. While 61 percent of senior management or higher say they are tightly aligned with sales and 54.7 percent say generally aligned.

162

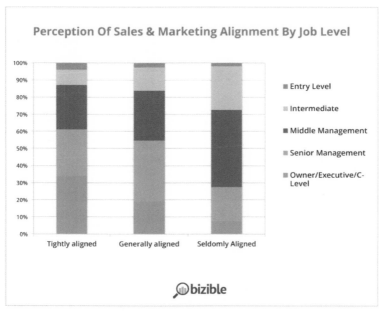

There are a couple takeaways here:

One, it seems that C-level execs understand the importance of aligning their marketing and sales teams, but this value gets lost as you move down the job ladder. And two, upper management may place value on overall revenue metrics while the lower job levels are more concerned with their job function metrics like leads and conversion rates. While those are also valuable, it's important for teams to be optimizing for the same metrics. Otherwise, it creates a marketing team that's not only siloed from sales, but also from each other, and it's easier to be successful when everyone is on the same page.

Sales and Marketing Alignment vs. Budget Over Next 12 Months

In the graph below, we find that 61.5 percent of marketers who are tightly aligned with sales expect their marketing budget to increase in the next 12 months. While only 3.13 percent expect it to decrease.

163

Of those who are rarely aligned (combines answers for "rarely" and "misaligned"), 62.9 percent say their budget will decrease or remain the same, while only 33.3 percent say it will increase.

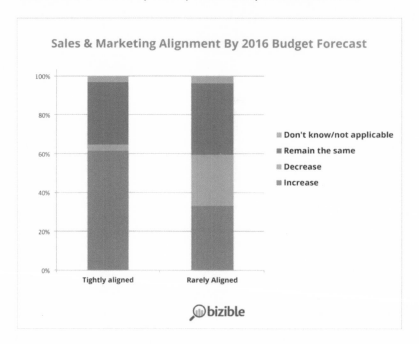

This tells us that when sales and marketing are aligned, they work better together as a team and it's paying off in terms of marketing budget growth, which of course supports sales. So not only does aligning with sales mean you're just more connected as a company, it can drive change and new business value as well.

Sales and Marketing Alignment vs. Primary Success Metric

Of those who answered as being tightly aligned with sales, 46.2 percent distributed their answers between two primary success metrics—total opportunities and total revenue. Those who answered within seldomly aligned had success metrics all over the board. Total leads took the slight edge as the primary success metric, coming in at 18.9 percent of the answers.

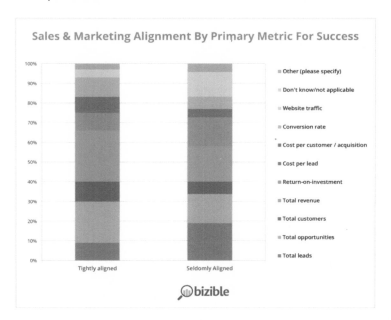

These results show that tight alignment between marketing and sales, means a more focused and unified measurement of success. Drawing a parallel, the metrics used to measure success are the same ones used as optimization goals. So, in the case of tightly aligned, marketing and sales teams are both interested in increasing total opportunities and total revenue.

Within the bar for seldomly aligned, the balanced distribution across multiple answers shows that when sales and marketing isn't aligned, teams may be optimizing and measuring for completely different metrics. Disjointed goals make it difficult to grow a business.

Overall, the report is showing that the more aligned sales and marketing are, the more positive results the team has— increased budget, more unified focus, and the ability to prove value to upper management.

Six Rules for More Effective Sales Lead Follow-Up

One week I highlighted some good and bad lead follow-up experiences I had first-hand. I listed a couple implications, but wanted to go deeper and get more specific on a few rules I believe constitute best practices for sales lead follow-up.

Document the best practice sequence (no matter how you define that)

Ask 10 inside sales managers and they'll give you 10 different lead follow-up sequences – # of touches, mix between email and phone, voicemail or no voicemail, etc.. No matter how you define it, make sure you have a consistent best practice sequence that's trained and reinforced throughout the organization.

Draft email templates and VM scripts

Give you smart, trained reps flexibility to customize their prospect messages, but give them a baseline template for each email as well as explicit script for voicemails. Ideally these include your best practices around messaging, format, offer, etc..

Diversify channels beyond email and phone

At minimum, your lead follow-up should include both email and phone/voicemail. Leaving voicemails has been proven to increase familiarity and awareness, which increases response rates of future outreach. But diversifying channels further will accelerate the path towards response. Think social, discussion boards, Twitter "favorites", LinkedIn Groups, their blog comments, anywhere you can generate a value-added impression with them that increases your engagement rate.

Automate and queue up the preferred outreach sequence as much as possible

Save those templates in Salesforce.com, or better yet queue them up as a Program in ToutApp. The advantage of the latter is real-time notification of opens and clicks, as well as rolled-up reporting on response rates, sales rep usage, etc.. This also helps save your reps time and increases their productivity.

Minimize recording and admin requirements for your reps

Speaking of productivity, make sure that increase in rigor and precision for the follow-up process doesn't come with an increase in administrative work for your reps. The more time they spend recording each and every voicemail, the less time they're actively selling.

Create a post-disposition nurture and trigger event program

Once your reps get through the full follow-up process without successfully reaching or qualifying the prospect (which will happen the majority of the time), develop a process that's more than just marking the lead as "nurture" and sending it back to marketing. Ask the rep to send a LinkedIn connection request, follow them on Twitter and watch their activity via a column in Hootsuite, as well as any other tactics that help your reps notice and respond to daily trigger events and buying signals your prospects exhibit down the road – tomorrow, next week, next month or later in the year.

When Do You Introduce Price in the Sales Process?

Price is tricky. It's one of those hard questions many sellers are worried about introducing at all, let alone too early such that it kills the deal.

You're worried they don't have budget. You want to believe they'll say yes anyway.

Budget is relative, of course. If they're in business, they have budget. They could cancel their lease or fire someone in order to afford you if the intended outcome were that important.

Price is different, but still relative to value. There's no such thing as an independent "that's too expensive" objection. Too expensive based on what?

If the cost of not buying is going out of business, what's too expensive? If the cost of not buying is that you'll lose some of your best employees or fail to win a big new contract, what's too expensive?

So it's not really a matter of *when* you introduce price, it's more about "with what" you introduce price.

If you haven't yet established the intended outcome your product or service represents, your prospect can't put that price in context.

If you haven't established that the intended outcome is urgent, that it's tied to a critical business objective or milestone, it's difficult to understand if your price is reasonable or justified.

If you pitch price while reinforcing a quantified value, you've done the math in advance for the prospect. You make it difficult to argue that achieving the outcome isn't worth paying a fraction of that for it.

Some use price at the very front of the sales process as a filtering mechanism. If they freak out about your proposed number without understanding what they are buying, is that really an objection to price? Or is it a lack of understanding of why or how they need what you're selling in the first place?

Along those lines, it's never too early to introduce price as long as it's in the context of value. And for that, the sooner the better.

The Hidden, Crippling Damage of Bad Sales Practices

You can make a spreadsheet say anything right?

You can hire people to make 100 dials a day, call prospects five times a week, push, push, push and make the numbers work out. With enough activity they'll get enough appointments, close enough deals, to help you make your number. Manage to the expectations in your spreadsheet model and everything will be fine.

Except....

Those reps may be calling too much, too often, pissing off prospects who now will never buy from you. Your brand is now associated with high-pressure sales reps, not anything to do with the value your product or service provides.

Your reps may be pitching product instead of communicating something of value, wasting the prospect's time vs. sharing something worth paying for. Multiply that by constant emails and voicemails that never stop and you're in trouble.

When your prospects recognize the phone number or area code every day, even without any interaction (or voicemail left), those passive interactions reinforce your growing, damaging brand value.

Your reps may be receiving direct, negative feedback on their tactics, but they sure aren't sharing that feedback with you. That'll make them look bad so they ignore it, delete it. You never see it.

If two percent of your prospects convert, that means 98 percent don't. And among those 98 percent, how many will never do business with you again? How many will tell their colleagues and peers about the experience? How many will forward that horrible email to their teammates, blog about it, tweet about it, talk about it?

How many will get promoted to manager, then director, then VP and beyond – and remember how you treated them?

The negative, long-term impact of bad sales practices is difficult to isolate and measure. But it's there. And I guarantee that your future spreadsheets will suffer for it without attention and course correction.

Are Great Salespeople Born or Made?

The answer, of course, is both.

Over the past couple years, I've found that the single-best indicator of a sales rep's likelihood of success in a new company is results from their personality and attribute tests. Past experience isn't always relevant. Hitting your number in a different industry (or sales era where the rules and tools were different) doesn't necessarily predict future success.

Fitting in with one company's culture doesn't mean they'll be a fit in yours.

That said, certain sales attributes tend to work across genres and cultures, regardless of past sales experience. Tenacity, rational optimism, discipline, collaboration tendencies. These skills can be trained, but some salespeople are just born with it. And on the other hand, some potential sales reps don't have it, and it's against their DNA to achieve it.

Sales skills can be trained. Sales process, tool usage, how to listen for buying signals. These skills can all be developed. And this very clearly isn't a pitch to devalue the importance of sales training in growing the skill set and success rate of your entire salesforce.

But certain skills that form the foundation of success for great salespeople are more inherent to their personalities, something they are going to bring to the table and your sales floor no matter how you train them.

Great salespeople can be made, but the consistently successful reps were born with the attributes that help make them great. If your hiring process doesn't yet account for this, you have some work to do.

172

A Sales and Marketing Alignment Checklist

Sales and marketing alignment is not a new concept. In fact, it has been pretty much beaten to death over the last few years with many marketing technology vendors claiming their product was the key to this Zen state.

Where has all that attention and investment left us?

Pretty much in the same place.

Sales and marketing alignment is more about process and people than enabling technology. Of course the technology can help automate tasks, create shared reports, and remove inefficiencies and workarounds but without the process aspect locked down and both sales and marketing leaders on the same page there is no alignment.

With that in mind, here is a 5 item Sales and Marketing Alignment Checklist you can put to work in your organization immediately:

1. **A shared "actual to plan" model mapping leads to customers and customers to revenue**

   This is not a new concept to sales leaders as they (should) live this view of their activities and accomplishments on a monthly or quarterly basis. What is a bit of a twist is having a marketing "actual to plan" model that parallels the sales plan and incorporates historical conversion rates so the number of qualified leads needed to generate the number of customers and accompanying revenue within the defined time period is known and tracked.

2. **An agreed upon definition of a Marketing Qualified Lead and Sales Qualified Lead**

Lead quality is the hot potato of sales and marketing alignment. It is frustrating for marketers to hear this when they work hard to generate interest and inquiries and it is frustrating for salespeople who struggle to engage and close leads that are barely more than a contact record.

Getting an agreed upon set of definitions in place and agreeing between groups to a Service Level Agreement (SLA) about qualification criteria, response time and recycling processes is essential. Print it out and have people sign it.

3. **A "Full Funnel" view of conversion rates and costs from lead to won or lost including month over month growth rates and quarterly/annual trends**

    Sales and marketing leaders must unite behind the funnel and own it collectively. It is a dynamic, complex, and living thing that must be constantly monitored and improved. Don't be afraid of the numbers. Embrace them and know how lead quality changes show up in the numbers or how investment in both sales and marketing efforts is actually paying off.

4. **A standing weekly meeting between the VP of Sales and VP of Marketing with a set agenda**

    Talk to each other – often. Have a standing meeting and even better if it is out of the office or early in the morning. Have a defined agenda that parallels this checklist. Communication is crucial to sales and marketing alignment and it starts at the top of the organization.

    Two different functional groups, usually compensated differently, creates a ripe situation for misunderstanding and conflict. Own it and resolve it. Speaking with one voice in the next executive team or board meeting is a powerful signal of complete alignment.

174

5. **An agile mindset to constantly challenge assumptions and improve the customer acquisition process**

   Know that sales and marketing alignment is a journey and not a destination. Continually challenge the assumptions being made about how customers buy or how the team finds, engages, and closes customers. Be open to new approaches and new techniques. Iterate often and create a tolerance for controlled experiments that can inform process changes and investment decisions.

   Sales and marketing alignment is not out of reach and using this checklist will go a long way towards getting aligned and becoming a customer acquisition machine.

Why Sales Still Doesn't Completely Trust Marketing

It's simple: At the end of the day, sales stands alone.

The marketing team may have the same objectives, on paper.

You may have common definitions between departments of qualified leads, qualified opportunities.

You have a common technology plan, integration between CRM and marketing automation.

The marketing team talks about revenue responsibility. And it all sounds good. It all sounds right.

But at the end of the month, the end of the quarter, who feels the terror? Who can't sleep at night? Who scrapes and claws to hit their number?

Marketing goes home, heads to happy hour, satisfied that they hit their lead number. Mission accomplished.

Meanwhile, their sales counterparts are making frenzied calls to get deals across the line, are pulling in favors to get a few more dollars in to make their quota.

This may not be an entirely fair comparison. There aren't many companies asking marketing to hit the phones, negotiate with procurement, literally push those last deals across the line.

It's not necessarily fair or rational. But when marketing claims revenue responsibility, yet abandons the sales team for their happy hour and "we hit our lead goal" celebrations, you can hopefully see where, and why, sales feels alone.

176

They've always been alone. On the last day of the month, it's the sales team that succeeds or fails. It's a fairly recent, new and refreshing trend for marketing to embrace revenue responsibility.

Just don't expect sales to trust so quickly, to believe without seeing you embrace and share the end-of-month terror regularly.

Thank you for the leads, the MQLs, the sales enablement initiatives. Are you there with us on the final lap, and at the finish line?

Productivity and Management

Do Your Meetings Need Meetings? The Secret to Productive Business Meetings

*By **Rebecca Smith**, Marketing Coordinator at Heinz Marketing*

Meetings that waste your time do more than just waste hours and minutes of your day, they lose your focus. Holding productive business meetings is really important to setting your attitude, organizing your to-do list and getting tasks accomplished. It's especially important to stay focused in the internal team meetings because that's where a lot of magic can happen. It's also the hardest place to stay focused...

You know your teammates well. You want to joke around and have a fun attitude. You don't want these meetings to be a bore... But, it's easy to forget you hold these meetings so you can be more productive in the long-term. Use this time well to soak up knowledge from your teammates and plan ahead accordingly.

To get through your busy day of meetings, follow these tips below.

What's our objective?

Ask this question before scheduling your meeting. What's the objective? Is this meeting about scheduling and planning? Strategic development? Brainstorming? Setting an objective at the beginning of the meeting will keep all parties involved focused on the task at hand. And, if it doesn't keep the group focused, at least you'll be focused thinking of how you're going to meet that objective in your short 30-minute time period...

Always set an agenda

Always, always, always. Agendas keep the group focused and corralled. Even if there are only two of you in a meeting, it's easy to get sidetracked (don't tell my boss, but I'm a frequent offender of this...) Agendas bring you back on track and ready to go.

Only invite the required

You want to invite the whole office because you know how awesome your colleagues are. They have great ideas. But, that doesn't mean they should join every meeting. Sometimes, more is merrier. In business meetings, more can be detrimental. Remember your objective—is Sally Sue really going to help me come to a conclusion and make this decision?

Wrap it up

Sheryl Sandberg, COO of Facebook, has this all dialed in. Once you've gone through your agenda, be like Sheryl and end the meeting. Don't sit around wasting time thinking you can goof off now that you're meeting is over. Why not put your effort into something more useful? And, I'm not saying get back to work right away. This could even mean taking the extra 15 minutes to go on a walk, clear your head, and refresh your thoughts.

Keep your phone out of sight, out of mind

Cell phones in meetings are dangerous territory. They ring so they distract you. They buzz so they distract you. Twitter notifies you of a new share, which distracts you. They are lean, mean distracting machines. If you aren't desperately waiting for a phone call, then leave them outside for your meeting time. It'll help keep you and your team thinking about the objective of the meeting instead of worried about what's going on in the Twittersphere.

While I know it sounds like more planning is needed to hold productive business meetings, the "extra" work I'm suggesting won't actually feel like extra work when you do it. To have an effective business meeting, just remember to think about your objective, set an agenda, only invite the required, keep it short and sweet, and leave your phone behind. Your meetings will seem more effective and much more manageable in no time.

The Routine vs. the Grind: Which Will You Choose?

I noticed something interesting as we slowly took down holiday decorations and got back to work in the new year.

This year I heard more people express how hard it was to get back into the swing of things starting that first Monday after New Years Day. That first day back was jarring, even depressing, for many. I admit I felt some of that as well.

But at the same time I heard many people express thanks for getting back into their "routine". We had some great visits from family during the holidays, but I personally enjoy a more normal daily routine – including more quiet time at night, more dedicated time to getting things done, etc..

There are certainly things outside of our control that aren't our favorite tasks or responsibilities. No matter who you are, or what job you have, there's work or roles that you don't look forward to.

But if we hate the grind but look forward to the routine, how do we minimize the former and accentuate the latter?

What specifically were you anxious about this past weekend? What were you NOT looking forward to heading into the first full work week of the New Year? If you can identify those specifically, how can you minimize or eliminate them?

This may be as simple as adjusting your priorities or focus areas, or as difficult as changing jobs or careers. But even if you're somewhere in the middle, why not name those anxious elements and decide if they really need to be a regular part of your life?

And conversely, what specifically about "the routine" do you appreciate and look forward to? Routine doesn't necessarily have to equate to a "rut" either. What are the things you get to do each day or week that gives you the most joy, the most satisfaction? And how do you pivot to do more of that moving forward?

Choosing your ideal routine, our explicit chosen priorities, may very well require short-term sacrifice. To do more of what you love may require changing your safe and comfortable routine, at least for now. But short-term change may be worth it if you're able to mitigate or eliminate "the grind" entirely.

Two Signs It's Time to Let an Employee Go

Fairly often in the course of working with clients we're in parallel asked to evaluate members of their sales and marketing team. This can be anyone from the VP of Sales to a junior marketing team member, with an expected variety of variables and criteria at play.

Evaluating measurable results is black and white, but deciding whether or not to let someone go often gets more gray than that. A good friend recently shared his criteria for knowing when it's time to move on from someone, even if they've been with you for a while.

Jordan Ritter is a successful start-up veteran currently running Ivy Softworks in Seattle. His focus is on an employee's reaction to feedback. In his words:

More specifically: It's time to part ways when either (1) someone can't hear critical feedback, or (2) they can't act upon it (can't change, evolve, grow, adapt).

For this to work, leadership must carry an extra burden around consistently managing via expectations, and articulating feedback clearly and constructively.

But the payoff is that people will always know where they stand. Even when the news is "bad", it still builds trust because what they hear from you jibes with what they feel, even if they can't admit it to themselves. This way they have an honest shot at improvement and growth, and the parting-ways conversation won't ever be a surprise when expectations are regularly unmet.

This combines ability with intent in an elegant way. Worth thinking about and leveraging as you evaluate staff at year-end and relative to your plans and objectives for the new year.

Seven Lessons I Learned From My Worst Boss Ever

I've actually been truly blessed with a long list of amazing bosses and mentors over the course of my career. I've learned so much about being a marketer, a business leader and a manager from bosses at Microsoft, start-ups and other stops in between.

But along that journey I had a short but very memorable experience which someone who was by far the worst boss I ever experienced. Thankfully, though, my time with her has given me some great lessons on what to do and what NOT to do as I continue learning how to be a better leader for my team.

Playing politics never pays

It's shallow, transparent and short-sighted. It may help you win the day, but it will lose you a ton of respect long-term with peers, superiors and subordinates.

Communicate clearly (not in code)

There's no excuse for allowing ambiguity to cloud judgement, direction or execution. If your style of management is to expect your team to predict or guess what you mean and want, that's terrible leadership. Not all news is good news, but people want clarity, not innuendoes.

Support your team (teach or correct them later)

Put your people in a position where they will learn, stretc.h their skills and comfort zones and limits, but give them a safety net. This includes giving them an opportunity to fail (and sometimes fail publicly) while reserving constructive feedback and redirection to more private, discrete opportunities.

Invest time with your team

Absentee management never works. You can't hide behind emails. And it's never a good idea to look annoyed when one of your team members wants to see you or ask you a question. Successful management requires time, it requires an investment in spending time with your team to make them better, allow them to become more autonomous and productive. That just takes time, but it creates results, loyalty and longevity (for you and for them).

Be clear about expectations

There's a difference between communicating clearly, and clarifying how your team will be evaluated and measured. It's OK if the metrics change, or the priorities change, but be clear when that happens, be clear that there will be time required to transition, and be clear that you are there to support them into those new objectives. I don't think I can use the word "support" enough in this blog post. It has many meanings, and they're all critical to driving clarity, morale and results with your team.

Superficial optics will backfire

This particular boss told us she wanted us to be at our desks as much as possible, so that people walking by would see how hard we are working. She literally said that to us. You can imagine what that did to her credibility.

Practice what you preach

There is one standard, not many.

10 Simple Habits to Jumpstart Your Productivity

You shouldn't be looking for quantum leaps of productivity. Rather, it's the little things – executed regularly – that will give you the boost in productivity you need to sell more, be more successful, and create more balance in your life.

Here are 10 habits I've found most valuable. All are simple in nature, yet difficult to execute regularly. Habits and discipline, man...

Wake up earlier

My alarm goes off every morning at 5:00 a.m. Some days I get up, some days I don't. Discipline that early is difficult for me, but if I do get up my day always goes better. I'm out the door on time, I'm not nearly as rushed, and often I can get a few things done early that give me a jump start on the day.

First thing's first (one of five)

Have your to-do list for the day, sure, but know what the #1 most important priority is for your day. Do that first. Yes, it's likely something gnarly, intimidating, not as much fun. But it's at the top of your list for a reason. Too often, getting #2-5 on your list done isn't nearly as important as #1.

Idea capture and triage

Your brain works much faster than you do. It'll have ideas all day long, but those ideas are fleeting if you don't write them down. Get in the habit of capturing more of your ideas and inspirations, then triage them later. The minority will be "do it now" ideas, some will be "file for later", some won't be relevant enough to keep. Separate capture and triage optimize quantity and quality.

188

Email discipline

Keep your email offline as much as possible. Focus as little time in your inbox as possible. 90 percent of your inbox is other people's priorities anyway. Get in, get out, get back to work.

Know your energy patterns

Everybody has different energy habits and patterns. For some, early morning is their best most productive time. For others, it's mid to late evening. Equally important is knowing when you typically have low energy. For me, that's early to midafternoon. I try not to schedule significant brain time work in that window, but know there's plenty of lower low-energy tasks and projects I can use that time for.

The Daily Do

Make yourself a checklist of the things you need to do on a regular basis. Most will become muscle memory, but the checklist is a safety net. This can be everything from writing, prospecting, lead follow-up, social media activity, whatever is important to you on a regular basis. For me, the "Daily Do" list changes often but it's a constant throughout the work week.

Two-minute rule

If it's in your inbox and takes two minutes or less to complete, do it right now. If it's not worth doing, get rid of it. If you don't have two minutes right now, you probably shouldn't be checking your email anyway!

Five-minute rule

Those intimidating projects usually aren't so bad once you get started. That's why I always give myself exactly five minutes to start something that's hard. After five minutes, it's typically not nearly as intimidating, plus I have a better sense for how long it's actually going to take to complete. And oftentimes, I just get it done right there and then.

Anytime tasks available anywhere

Keep a constant list of things you can think about or brainstorm with you at all times. For me, I keep these in my Outlook Tasks (available via TaskTask on my iPhone) sorted with the @Anywhere tag. This can be anything – brainstorming blog post content, thinking through a new marketing strategy, making a weekend project list, etc.. Little pockets of time throughout the day (waiting in line, for example) can become little pockets of productivity.

Take care of yourself (sleep, exercise, rest)

Get enough sleep. Exercise. Let your brain rest. Watch stupid television from time to time. Find a hobby that's diametrically different from what you do all day. Recharging is a critical part of being more productive when you're intently working.

The Power and Importance of a Weekly Review (and How I Do It)

I could argue that the single-most important thing I do all week to keep myself focused and productive is the weekly review.

My process is based on the more extensive Weekly Review (capitalization added for emphasis and importance) in David Allen's *Getting Things Done* system. My version is a bit shorter, but in my opinion still highly valuable and easier to emulate (as well as stick with on a regular basis).

It starts with a comprehensive inventory of projects. I keep these in Outlook Tasks tagged as "Projects – Active". For me, a project is anything that's more than one task. Something I can't or won't get done right away.

These projects cover a lot of ground. All work-related projects (for the business, for clients, for staff, etc..), all household projects, things I need to do in my personal life, etc.. I use this as a safety net to keep track of all the more comprehensive things I want to get done. Oftentimes, if I come up with a project in the middle of the week that doesn't need to be worked on right away, I'll add it to the Project list and literally "forget about it" until the next weekly review.

I do also have a "Projects – Someday" list that's full of things I eventually want to do. I typically review this list quarterly to see if anything needs to be moved to the Active list.

So, Sunday night. Dinner, get kids to bed, pour a nice little Scotch.

I print out that Active Projects list so I have it physically in front of me. I have it alphabetized by topic so it's easier to work through. For example, something that's a Heinz Marketing project might be titled

"Heinz Marketing: Holiday Party Planning". Sometimes a project will have notes included or attached, sometimes not.

Then, with Scotch in hand, I work through each Project on the list one by one. At each step, I do one of the following:

Identify an immediate next steps for my task list: If it's something I haven't worked on yet or in awhile, I quickly identify the immediate next thing I need to do – the tactical, single next task – to move that project forward. Typically, this gets assigned to myself as a to-do later in the week. I don't worry about whatever task comes after that. This usually gets notated once the first task is complete, or there's next week's review to pick it back up again.

Make a note to ask for an update on something I'm waiting for: Sometimes I'm waiting for a deliverable or update from someone else, and the weekly review helps me remember to ask for and get that more quickly.

Confirm (on paper or in my head) that I already have the right next step in my task list: Self-explanatory.

Defer to next week: This happens quite often. Many things on my active project list just aren't going to get attention in the coming week given other priorities. In this case, I give myself permission to literally forget about it until the following week's review

Delete the project: If it's been completed, it's gone. Sometimes projects get moved to the "someday" folder, but most of the time they stay active until they are completed.

What results from this is typically a fairly full to-do list for the coming week. But it gives me confidence that I'm focusing on the right things, and not letting anything fall through the cracks.

192

During the week, new projects get added. Sometimes that comes with an immediate first to-do on my task list, sometimes I just wait until the next weekly review.

I think of this as my weekly safety net. If I'm focused, I can typically get this done in 30 minutes or so.

Work Ethic

It's not about working the most hours, or sending the most emails, replying to everything, showing off that you're working Sunday or late nights or even on holidays.

Work ethic isn't about spending the most time at the office, or as much time as possible in front of a screen.

Work ethic is about discipline. Consistency. Results.

It's about putting in what it takes to get the job done, and get it done right.

Those with a strong work ethic care about what they're doing, they care about how it looks and how it performs. They care about quality, craftsmanship.

Work ethic is not about reputation. It is not about ego. It is not about getting in earlier or staying later than everybody else.

Work ethic is often associated with a LOT of work. Lots of work is what's required to succeed. There are no shortcuts.

But work ethic is not about the work. It's about how you work, and what you produce. It's about how you approach the work, how you stick with the work, and how you complete the work.

It's not a race, or a contest, or a beauty contest. You don't have work ethic because you brag about work ethic.

Do the work. Do it right. Do it until it is finished. Work until you are satisfied with the results.

No less. That is work ethic.

The Seven Habits of Highly-Effective B2B Marketers

I've been thinking a lot lately about what makes for a great B2B marketer. As we grow the Heinz Marketing team, as well as help our clients evaluate new talent, I'm looking for a mix of experience, hard skills and values. Here are seven areas I've found really matter.

1. Revenue responsibility

Marketing needs to act like a profit center, with a direct orientation towards sales pipeline and revenue contribution. This means more than just alignment with sales goals. It means making daily decisions, sometimes hard decisions, about where to focus and what to execute based on revenue impact. This is easier said than done, but is critical (and is at the top of the list for a reason).

2. Focus

I think of this as a combination of planning and triage. No successful marketer that I know works without a plan, but best-laid plans rarely survive first contact with the battlefield. It's how great marketers react to those changes, those new environmental conditions, those initiatives that succeed or fail, that separates the successful from mediocre professionals. You spend most of your time in triage, but it's impossible to stay focused without a plan.

3. Persona driven

I ask two questions at the beginning of any new project, engagement or initiative. One, how are we measuring success? Two, who the heck are we selling to and why do they care? You can spend months and tens of thousands of dollars building detailed personas. Or, you can listen to your customers. Your customer-facing employees. Understand not what they're buying but why. What problem are they solving, what need are they fulfilling, what story are they telling themselves that you align with.

4. Personal accountability and productivity

This goes well beyond being busy and productive. Yes, a disciplined approach to email, time and task list is important. But this also means being accountable for how that time affects your output. How effectively you're staying focused on what matters. No excuses, just problem solving and execution.

5. Technology balance

Don't let the tail wag the dog. There's plenty of sexy technology out there, but make sure you have a strategy first.

6. An agile mentality

Great marketers have a higher tolerance for chaos. They accept that change is not only inevitable, but frequent and necessary. They also have a high degree of humility, which often manifests itself in a strong sense of humor and even self-deprecation.

7. Empathy

For each other, for the sales organization, for other departments, for your customers. Sometimes it's just asking the other side what's important to them, what they need, or how they're feeling. Empathy is a powerful thing, a powerful negotiation tool, and an amazing emotional trigger that unlocks so much more potential and output from those around you.

Anxiety as an Obstacle or a Motivator (and Sometimes Both)

I have generalized anxiety. I think I've had it for years, going back to my childhood, but it really came to a head about eight years ago. I'd get anxious about a lot of things, but especially travel and bad weather. Put me halfway across the country with a delayed flight and pending snow storm and I would have a hard time functioning.

Come to find out, a lot more people struggle with anxiety than I thought. Through working with a fantastic psychiatrist and some baseline meds, I've been able to get anxiety far better under control the past several years.

Someone who also struggles with anxiety once described their anxiety as an old, cranky friend. Even if you have it generally under control, it's still there.

And although anxiety has been an obstacle in my life at times, I believe strongly that it has also been a motivator. Anxiety exists in us for a reason, so that our senses are heightened to potential danger to keep us *out* of danger. You don't really want to eliminate anxiety from your life for that reason, but you want to make sure it doesn't keep you from functioning, from living freely, from enjoying life.

Without anxiety we might not perceive danger as well as we should. That includes physical danger as well as the fear of missing your number, missing your flight, missing your mortgage payment.

Anxiety is a form of fear, and fear is a powerful motivator. But that fear can focus you or debilitate you.

Anxiety can focus you on the task at hand. Or it can distract you beyond the ability to execute anything.

Anxiety is a natural human condition, but something you can focus for good. Anxiety can help you achieve results you didn't previously think possible. It can scare you into success.

It's a slippery slope. It's clearly playing with fire.

But thus far I've come to terms with my anxiety. It still scares me. But I don't think I would have achieved what I have so far without it.

Five Simple Rules to Maximize Your Next Business Trip, Conference or Event

I'd argue that these apply equally to conferences, small gatherings, offsite, team meetings and more:

Go in with a plan: Decide in advance what sessions you are prioritizing, where you want to be throughout the day. This plan is your guide, not your master. It's your default priority, with permission to change at any time.

Meet as many people as possible: Sitting next to you at the general session, in line for food, in the hotel elevator. If they're wearing the same badge around their neck, they are one of you.

Be open to serendipity: An unexpected meeting, a spontaneous invitation. These impromptu opportunities often become the highlight of your trip with the longest-tail of value, personally and professionally.

Take tons of notes: A great event is like a fire hose of ideas – some direct, some inspired, some simply triggering something independent, irrelevant but critical to your life, your business, your career, your objectives. Your best chance at leveraging those ideas is to capture as many as possible, giving you time to reflect and act on more of them later.

Be present: If you insist on checking email every 10 minutes, keeping every regularly-scheduled conference call, getting just as much "at office" work done as usual, you'll fail to benefit from being truly out of the office. This is your chance to learn something new, meet someone inspiring, get a spark that makes that back-at-the-office work far more compelling, valuable and successful. Sometimes the best conferences begin with the best preparation. Clear your schedule, get work done before or plan to get it done later. Be there in mind and body.

You Can't Work Yourself Out of Work

There will always be more work. You have to prioritize, focus...and stop.

You can't work all day, all weekend. You'll drive yourself crazy, and you still won't be done.

People who tell me they're too busy to take a vacation, or even to take the weekend off, are taking themselves far too seriously. None of us are that important.

One of our directors is taking three weeks off this summer, starting yesterday. She was crazy busy last Friday and she'll be crazy busy when she gets back. In the meantime, she's doing zero work on a variety of beaches in Spain and Greece.

It doesn't make her less valuable. It doesn't make her less important. Sometimes a sign of someone's value and contribution isn't how hard they work, but how well they prepare to *not* work. How well they empower those around them. How they make themselves redundant, replaceable. How they use time *not* working to improve their focus, energy and productivity when they *are* working.

You'll never be able to work so hard that you actually finish the work, so stop *well* before that point and focus instead on the right work. Work hard, but work smart.

Easy in theory, very difficult in practice. But worth it.

How to Keep an Empty Desk and Still Get a Ton Done

I love a clean work surface. It helps me stay focused, and keeps me productive with minimal distractions. I know that for some, visual reminders are critical. I used to be that way too. Ten years ago, my desk was an absolute mess.

And I'd easily get distracted by something out of the corner of my eye, or focus on something that was urgent or fun or easy without triaging and prioritizing the important stuff first.

Now, my desk top at work and at my home office is as clean as possible, as often as possible. At work, that typically means dual monitors, a keyboard and mouse, a digital picture frame....and that's about it. At home it's not much different.

Keeping such a clean desk, and still getting a ton done, takes a fair amount of discipline and process. But since I'm traveling and away from my desk often, it also helps ensure that I always have with me the things necessary to get almost anything done.

Here are a few best practices that have been particularly helpful for me:

Processing Discipline: I take notes with pen and paper, but quickly thereafter convert action items, ideas and immediate to-do's into tasks in Outlook, lists in Evernote or reminders in my calendar. If too much time passes between note-taking and processing, it's too easy to 1) forget about something, 2) not get it done quickly enough, and 3) let it get piled up with other meeting notes and to-do's. Quick and consistent triage is key.

Task Lists in the Cloud: I use Outlook Tasks for 90% of my action items. Some of my lists (especially for household projects, weekend honey-do lists and errands – think grocery store and Home Depot

202

runs) have migrated to Evernote as well. But it's all available on every device, and it's all digital. It may start on paper, but it's stored and completed online.

All Paper Becomes Digital: Correspondence, hand-written notes, handouts from meetings – I convert it all into PDFs and store it in our Box system. This eliminates a ton of paper (which gets cluttered and also can reside in only one physical location) and makes it really easy to access information later. For example, in a meeting earlier today I was able to reference notes taken three months earlier – and it took me less than 10 seconds to call up those notes on my laptop. Love it (yes I'm geeking out on this, but you're still reading...)

Organized Drawers: I previously would keep things on my desk not only as reminders but so that I didn't lose them when I needed them next. This included staplers, pens, etc.. Now I keep a fairly disciplined way of storing these things in desk drawers both at home and at the office. This way I know exactly where to find something without needing it visible all the time.

Two Screens: I'm writing this on my laptop, but when working from my office or home desk I use two screens not only to increase reading/working space, but also to use the second screen as an alternative to paper. This works especially well when I'm referencing previous notes or something that has already been scanned into a digital format.

A (Temporary) Physical Inbox: OK, there is one more thing on my desk. It's a physical, wire inbox. New items to "process" go in that inbox. And given everything you've read above, you can guarantee it drives me NUTS to have stuff in there. Even further motivation to process through it and make an immediate decision how to handle – do, delegate, defer or delete. This too takes discipline to process on a regular basis, but I find it goes very quickly if I keep myself from getting distracted.

Geeky? Perhaps. Overkill? Maybe. But it works for me....

15 Minutes to Clear Your Head and Discover New Ideas

At some point before the end of the week, give this a shot.

Turn off your computer, put your phone in airplane mode, shut the door. Isolate yourself with no distractions.

Put a pen and paper in front of you on a desk. And shut your eyes.

If you're meditating at this point, you're trying to still your brain and thoughts. But I actually want you to try the opposite.

Let your brain go where it goes. Use the pen and paper to write down whatever comes up.

David Allen calls this a brain-dump at the beginning of his *Getting Things Done (GTD)* process. There are tons of ideas, projects and tasks in your head that simply need to be documented in a trusted system.

Whether or not you've used the GTD system is beside the point here. Even if you use GTD or a similar system, I bet you rarely sit quietly and let your brain think for you.

I don't do this often enough. The random but important things that come up in my 15 minutes of quiet often surprise me. Everything from blog post ideas to errands to gift ideas for the kids to client opportunities etc.. The mundane may save you and the breakthroughs will inspire you.

Will You Treat End of Year as a Finish line or a Race Buddy?

During Q4 many companies are entering the stretch run to finish the year strong. You set goals (financial and otherwise) in January and need to hit or exceed those objectives by the end of December.

But December 31st isn't really a finish line. Yes, you need to hit your number. But it's also a buoy, a milestone towards the next stage of success.

For example, in yacht racing, each boat must navigate the race course by making their way around a set of buoys set at various intervals. If the boat makes a direct line to the buoy, they'll likely be on an immediate course *away* from the next buoy. Smart captains know the best way to finish the race quickly is to angle *around* the buoy so that you hit the milestone but give yourself the best trajectory towards the next buoy.

Same goes for baseball. If you're trying to stretch a single into a double, you'd better not run straight through first base. If you take the turn correctly, you'll get to second faster, even though your time to first may be slower than running straight through.

My point is this – know that December is an important milestone and hitting your number counts for a lot. But your objectives for January and next year will come right after, and likely be more challenging. Hit your number this year, but find a way to take the turn around that milestone with trajectory and momentum into January and beyond.

Credits and Copyrights

You can find more information on much of the contents of this book, as well as additional information and insights, at www.heinzmarketing.com/blog.

We hope the best practices in this book inspire you to think differently about how marketing can impact your organization, your sales and your revenue results. We are constantly learning from the very best B2B marketing has to offer, and were particularly inspired by people such as Jill Konrath, Trish Bertuzzi, Steve Richard, Keenan, Ann Handley, Jay Baer, David Meerman-Scott, David Brock, Craig Rosenberg, Dan Waldschmidt, Anthony Iannarino, Scott Brinker, Tiffani Bova, Sean Burke, Lori Richardson, Joe Pulizzi, Michael Brennan and many, many others.

Special thanks to the entire Heinz Marketing team for writing, contributing to and inspiring this book. Extra special thanks to Sheena McKinney for her tireless work, dedication to service and details (you have no idea....), to Nicole Williams for her design work on the cover, and to Kailee McKinney, Lydia Yekalam, and Sheena McKinney for their editing and proofreading.

About the Author

Matt Heinz brings more than 15 years of marketing, bus and sales experience from a variety of organizations, vert company sizes. His career has focused on delivering measu his employers and clients in a way of greater sales, revenue g success and customer loyalty.

Matt has held various positions at companies such as Microso Shandwick, Boeing, The Seattle Mariners, Market Leader and Ver 2007, Matt began Heinz Marketing to help clients focus their busin market and customer opportunities, then execute a plan to scale rev and customer growth. Matt lives in Kirkland, Washington with his wife, Be three children and a menagerie of animals (a dog, a cat, and six chickens).

Heinz Marketing Blog
www.heinzmarketing.com/blog

LinkedIn Profile
www.linkedin.com/in/mattheinz

Matt's Business
www.heinzmarketing.com

Matt on Twitter
www.twitter.com/heinzmarketing